D0386638

ADVANCE PRAISE FOR
WIKI MANAGEMENT:

"Rod Collins's new book, *Wiki Management,* is one of the simplest and clearest explanations of the principles and practices of the emerging new management paradigm for the 21st Century."

—Stephen Denning, author of *The Leader's Guide to Radical Management*

"This is the THE leaders' handbook for the 21st century. Read it and begin putting to work the most powerful management practices available today. Collins is lucid, easy to understand and apply. He gets it right. Every leader should buy this book, then buy it for their cabinet and all their managers. I recommend it unreservedly."

—Seth Kahan, author of *Getting Innovation Right*

"A couple of decades from now, we will look back to this time as a time of transformation, the time when we first groped for new methods to replace the management principles—used since the birth of professional management—but no longer sufficient to assure success in the face of unrelenting business uncertainty. From this future perspective, we will see Rod Collins as a pioneer, uncovering new management tenets as they first emerged. In a couple of decades everyone will use the wiki style of management, but why wait? Read Rod's book and you can start now."

—Charlie Rudd, CEO, SolutionsIQ

"Rod Collins captures the essence of a new management model for the future. In our rapidly changing world, it is up to us in management to 'get on the right bus.' With specific guidance through many practical practices, Rod shows us exactly how to make the transition from older, antiquated management styles to a new collaborative, team-oriented style. Executives and managers who are looking to steer their companies effectively in the turbulent future will find this book an invaluable companion on the ride."

—Sanjiv Augustine, author of *Managing Agile Projects* and President, LitheSpeed, LLC

"Rod Collins is one of the few thought leaders who not only 'gets' how the world is changing but, more importantly, what businesses must do to succeed in today's fast-paced and complex world. I love the roadmap and powerful practices that any leader can use to transform his or her organization."

—Roger K. Allen, Ph.D., President, The Center for Organizational Design

"*Wiki Management* is a must-read for managers who know the future is no longer a projection of the past. The many practical cases and concrete practices described throughout the book give managers a valuable orientation so they may promote the much-needed management paradigm shift within their organizations."

—Franz Röösli, coauthor of *The Leader's Dilemma*

"I recommend *Wiki Management* to top managers, entry managers, and every management level in between. As the former chief operating executive for one of the most complex health insurance entities in the world, Rod Collins draws upon his extensive first-hand experience to provide clear and instructive insights into how the most nimble organizations achieve success in today's rapidly changing markets."

—Steven S. Martin, President & CEO, Blue Cross Blue Shield of Nebraska

"*Wiki Management* is a practical guide for moving beyond the command-and-control management model. Rod Collins provides a comprehensive framework and complements it with a set of management practices for day-to-day application based on actual experiences from vanguard companies. 'It can be done' is a key message that should resonate with managers who struggle at the intersection of the old and new worlds of management."

—Richard Straub, President, Peter Drucker Society, Europe

Collins, Rod, 1941–
Wiki management : a
revolutionary new model
[2014]
3 305 2036361066
cu   02/28/14

WIKIMANAGEMENT

A REVOLUTIONARY NEW MODEL FOR A RAPIDLY
CHANGING AND COLLABORATIVE WORLD

Rod Collins

AMACOM

AMERICAN MANAGEMENT ASSOCIATION

New York • Atlanta • Brussels • Chicago • Mexico City • San Francisco
Shanghai • Tokyo • Toronto • Washington, D.C.

Bulk discounts available. For details visit: www.amacombooks.org/go/specialsales
Or contact special sales: Phone: 800-250-5308 E-mail: specialsls@amanet.org
View all the AMACOM titles at: www.amacombooks.org
American Management Association: www.amanet.org

This publication is designed to provide accurate and authoritative information in regard to the subject matter covered. It is sold with the understanding that the publisher is not engaged in rendering legal, accounting, or other professional service. If legal advice or other expert assistance is required, the services of a competent professional person should be sought.

LIBRARY OF CONGRESS CATALOGING-IN-PUBLICATION DATA
Collins, Rod, 1941–
Wiki management : a revolutionary new model for a rapidly changing and
collaborative world / Rod Collins.
pages cm
Includes bibliographical references and index.
ISBN-13: 978-0-8144-3308-9
ISBN-10: 0-8144-3308-1
1. Management. 2. Organizational change. 3. Technological innovations—Management.
I. Title.
HD31.C6135 2014
658—dc23   2013017858

© 2014 Rod Collins
All rights reserved.
Printed in the United States of America.

This publication may not be reproduced, stored in a retrieval system, or transmitted in whole or in part, in any form or by any means, electronic, mechanical, photocopying, recording, or otherwise, without the prior written permission of AMACOM, a division of American Management Association, 1601 Broadway, New York, NY 10019.

The scanning, uploading, or distribution of this book via the Internet or any other means without the express permission of the publisher is illegal and punishable by law. Please purchase only authorized electronic editions of this work and do not participate in or encourage piracy of copyrighted materials, electronically or otherwise. Your support of the author's rights is appreciated.

About AMA

American Management Association (www.amanet.org) is a world leader in talent development, advancing the skills of individuals to drive business success. Our mission is to support the goals of individuals and organizations through a complete range of products and services, including classroom and virtual seminars, webcasts, webinars, podcasts, conferences, corporate and government solutions, business books, and research. AMA's approach to improving performance combines experiential learning—learning through doing—with opportunities for ongoing professional growth at every step of one's career journey.

Printing number
2 4 6 8 10 9 7 5 3 1

To Meghan and Melissa

Contents

Preface   ix

Acknowledgments   xv

1. Getting on the Right Bus   3

2. Letting Go of an Old Mindset   27

3. Resetting the 3 M's   53

4. Understand What's Most Important to Customers   75

5. Aggregate and Leverage Collective Intelligence   99

6. Build Shared Understanding by Bringing Everyone
   Together in Open Conversations   123

7. Focus on the Critical Few Performance Drivers   149

8. Hold People Accountable to Their Peers   171

Epilogue   199

Notes   205

Index   213

Preface

Today's managers face a difficult and unprecedented challenge: The world is changing much faster than their organizations. Every industry, without exception, has been overtaken by an accelerating pace of change that shows no signs of letting up anytime soon. In a business world of increasing uncertainty, the one clear certainty is that the pace of change is only going to get faster.

As managers struggle to keep pace with a fast-forward world, they are increasingly becoming aware of a very troubling problem. They are discovering that methods and practices that have always delivered predictable results aren't working anymore. Forecasts are suddenly unreliable as new disruptive technologies radically reshape markets. Cutting costs does not necessarily result in improved efficiencies and productivity. Proven analytical methods are now too slow and cumbersome to keep up with a fast-changing world. And exerting more control seems to drive companies out of control—and sometimes out of business. In a world where change is constant and longstanding rules don't seem to work anymore, it's not surprising that many managers feel overwhelmed by what appears to be a completely unmanageable state of affairs.

At the same time, there is a small but growing group of vanguard companies that is thriving in this time of great change. While most companies have had to trim their sails to weather the storm of the Great Recession, this small group has experienced relatively smooth sailing with steady growth, increasing profits, and the creation of new jobs. The vanguard group, composed of companies that we love engaging with as consumers, includes Amazon, Google, Threadless, Valve, Whole Foods, and Zappos, among others. What separates these vanguard companies from their traditional counterparts is that their managers understand a fast-changing world is not necessarily unmanageable—it just needs to be managed differently. That's because, with the rapid emergence of the Digital Age, we suddenly find ourselves in a new world with a completely different set of rules. The managers of the vanguard companies are thriving because they have mastered these new rules, and in so doing, they have completely overhauled the fundamental disciplines of business management.

While most of us are aware of the much-publicized successes of these vanguard companies, few of us are familiar with how they achieve their extraordinary performance. We have a vague notion that they do things a little differently, but chances are most of us would be surprised at just how differently the leaders of these companies manage their businesses. In fact, if we spent a week inside one of these innovative enterprises, most of us probably would walk away puzzled at how they could be so successful when we didn't see anything that remotely resembled management.

For most of us, management is about business plans, organization charts, bosses, formal meetings, policies, procedures, tasks, and reports. These are the common practices of the top-down hierarchical structures that have defined the context of management for well over a century. These practices are the embodiment of a fundamental set of disciplines that have served as the framework for leading and managing large organizations. This framework dates back to the late nineteenth century, when mass production was radically transforming the ways people worked and the major challenge for managers was how to effectively coordinate the tasks and activities of the large numbers of workers in their new factories.

Management, as most of us know it, was invented to guide business leaders in building and preserving sustainable business models and maintaining highly efficient operations. Its disciplines were designed to support the core values of top-down hierarchical structures: planning, control, and efficiency. Accordingly, in the command-and-control management model, the fundamental work of the manager is to plan and control, and productivity is synonymous with efficiency.

The managers of the vanguard companies, however, loathe command-and-control management. In fact, they are quite proactive in making sure that as their organizations grow, they do not inadvertently slip into traditional management practices. Instead, they have created a different management model that is based on a completely different set of fundamental disciplines. This alternative model is designed for adapting and innovating rather than preserving and maintaining. Its disciplines support the prime values of learning, collaboration, and innovation. Thus, the fundamental work of the manager is not to plan and control but rather to be the catalyst for collective learning and collaboration. And productivity is seen more as a function of innovation than efficiency.

The managers of the vanguard companies see little value in making traditional business models faster or less expensive. The real value is in creating the new business model that will render the old model obsolete. That's why, when the vanguard managers think about productivity, they focus on value rather than cost. When it comes to improving the bottom line, creating value is far more efficient than cutting costs.

This book is about the emerging management model used by the vanguard companies to make sure that their organizations are changing as quickly as the world around them. We call this new model "Wiki Management." *Wiki* is the Hawaiian word for "quick" or "fast," and it is an appropriate appellation for a set of management disciplines designed to help managers keep pace with accelerating change. In the chapters ahead, we will describe the five specific disciplines that the vanguard companies share in common, and we will outline fifty concrete practices that they use to drive their extraordinary performance. As you read through the book and become familiar with the new management model, please keep an open mind because many of these practices will feel counterintuitive, some will seem heretical, and most will probably challenge your basic assumptions about what managers do and what management is.

Although there is some discussion of the theory that serves as the foundation for the new management model, the bulk of the book is devoted to stories and practices. When managers are ready to think and act differently, real stories of success and actual practices that work are more valuable than abstract theory. Some of the stories and practices come from the vanguard companies referenced above, while others reflect my own experiences as a manager building a Wiki Management business unit inside a larger, traditional enterprise, and how we used many of the practices to quickly and successfully turn around a business that had endured two decades of low growth and low performance.

In our case, we learned the disciplines of Wiki Management out of necessity when we realized that the prime enabler of our poor performance was our adherence to a traditional management model that no longer worked. Learning new ways of managing wasn't easy because we needed to readjust the deeply held beliefs we had about what managers do and what management is. However, if we were going to improve our performance, we knew we had to change, regardless of how unfamiliar or counterintuitive managing differently might feel. Our venture into Wiki Management transformed us into a highly effective management team and enabled us to realize the single largest five-year growth period in the fifty-three-year history of our business unit. In embracing the new management model, we didn't just turn the business around; like so many of the vanguard companies, we made a leap to extraordinary performance.

The primary message of this book is simple and, hopefully, obvious: A nineteenth-century management model is unsustainable in a twenty-first-century world. As the pace of change continues to accelerate, it is unrealistic to believe that a century-old management model will somehow endure while the rest of the world is reshaped by the technologies of the Digital Age. We live in a new world with new rules, and the old rules are quickly becoming obsolete. That's why they're not working anymore.

As you approach this book, be prepared to be surprised because everything you have believed about the way we work and the work we do is about to dramatically change. In the chapters ahead, you will discover a very different business world where leaders are facilitators, workers are highly involved in shaping strategic thinking, and business processes are designed around what's most important to customers. You will become familiar with a new management vocabulary that describes the innovative tools of twenty-first-century business: serendipity, emergence, collective intelligence, shared understanding, simple rules, and self-organization. But most importantly, you will have at your disposal a set of fifty specific practices that you can use to master the unprecedented challenges of our fast-changing world. While fifty practices may sound like a lot, you'll find that you will be able to pick out those that are best suited to your particular business or situation. I hope that you will find much value in these pages and will commit to discovering and applying the incredible power of the disciplines and the practices of Wiki Management so you too can make a leap to extraordinary performance.

Rod Collins
rod.collins@optimityadvisors.com
www.optimityadvisors.com
Aurora, Colorado
November 2013

Acknowledgments

In many ways, writing a book is analogous to running a marathon. Each is a quest that requires diligent preparation, a healthy sense of self-discipline, and support from many people during the actual journey. Marathons would be lonely endeavors without the companionship of fellow runners, the encouragement of the event volunteers, and the cheers from many spectators along the way. The same has been true in writing this book. I have had the privilege of sharing this adventure with many remarkable people, some through their constant presence, others through our work together, and still others through the wisdom of their written words. However our paths have crossed, I am deeply indebted to all of them for their ideas and contributions.

I am particularly grateful to all my many friends and colleagues in the Blue Cross and Blue Shield organizations throughout the United States for their commitment and dedication in serving the millions of customers in the Federal Employee Program. Though there is not enough space to acknowledge each of them individually, I am forever enriched because they are the ones who first showed me the incredible power of collective intelligence and taught me that nobody is smarter than everybody.

I would like to give special thanks to my colleagues at Optimity Advisors for their constant support, especially Rick McNabb, whose passion for innovation and commitment to the power of collaboration made this book possible.

Many thanks to the following people for investing hours in reading parts of the manuscript, discussing its underlying principles, providing feedback, and helping me think more clearly about the concepts and the practices in this book: Anne Murray Allen, Roger Allen, Sanjiv Augustine, Virginia Avrutin, John Balkcom, Rose Marie Barbeau, Bill Barberg, Bill Beausay, Dave Block, Amber Bray, Dennis Carrai, Larry Cooper, Shane Cragun, Rob Creekmore, Stephen Denning, Kelly Dwight, Toby Gallegos, Glenna Gerard, Lester Jenkins, Dawna Jones, Seth Kahan, Lisa Kimball, Henri Lipmanowicz, Wendy Mack, Mike Mazza, Keith McCandless, Reed Meyer, Dan Montgomery, Stephanie Nestlerode, Aaron Ninness, Tom Ninness, Jeanette Nyden, Jim Parker, Fred Plumb, Don Prentice, Lew Rhodes, Ed Smith, Michael Spayd, Peter Stevens, Kevin Stoffel, John Stypulkoski, Bob Tobias, Mary Walewski, Dave Weaver, and Robert White.

I am also indebted to the many intellectual pioneers whose writings have opened me to the innovative ways of thinking and acting that are hastening the arrival of the wiki world: Ken Auletta, Rod A. Beckstrom, Josh Bernoff, Ori Brafman, John Seely Brown, Steven Cabana, James Champy, Ram Charan, Clayton Christensen, Jim Collins, Sean Covey, Lang Davison, Thomas L. Friedman, John Hagel III, Gary Hamel, Michael Hammer, Dee Hock, Jeff Howe, Tony Hsieh, Jim Huling, Jeff Jarvis, A. G. Lafley, Polly LaBarre, Steven Levy, Charlene Li, Andrew Lih, John Mackey, Chris McChesney, Peter Miller, Melanie Mitchell, Richard Ogle, Harrison Owen, Ronald E. Purser, Eric Raymond, Fred Reichheld, Peter M. Senge, Raj Sisodia, James Surowiecki, Don Tapscott, William C. Taylor, Margaret J. Wheatley, and Anthony D. Williams.

I would like to express special appreciation to my agent, Sandra Bond, who has enthusiastically believed in the message of this book and provided invaluable support and assistance. Without her passion and dedication, this book would not exist.

Kudos as well to Christina Parisi, executive editor of AMACOM Books, who provided the vision that made this a far better book than it would have otherwise been. She and her outstanding team exceeded every expectation.

Finally, I am deeply thankful to my family for their constant love, support, and inspiration. It is my great fortune to share my journey with my wife, Catherine. Her unwavering faith and encouragement has been my greatest blessing on this quest. I've learned so much about our new world and its new rules from hours of rich conversations with our daughters, Melissa and Meghan, and their spouses. I am grateful for their patience and tutoring in showing me how fast the world is changing. I am inspired by the joy and curiosity of our three wonderful grandsons, who are true children of our new wiki world. They give me hope that our best times are yet to come.

WIKIMANAGEMENT

1

Getting on the Right Bus

I n the late 1990s, the recording industry was in the midst of an incredible financial bonanza when a whole generation of music lovers happily replaced their vinyl album collections with superior-quality compact discs. With the development of an essentially scratch-free technology, the CD appeared to be the proverbial golden goose that would keep on giving. After nearly a century, the industry appeared to have mastered the challenge of creating the perfect record album. If you were a manager in either the production or the retailing of music in the last decade of the twentieth century, your business fortunes were looking very favorable.

Unfortunately, unexpected events can change things very quickly, as the music executives discovered with the onset of the new millennium. Beginning in 2001, their cozy world was shaken by the equivalent of a seismic shock when an unknown college student working in his dorm room created the file-sharing platform Napster, and large numbers of music lovers started swapping individual songs over the Internet. Why buy bundled songs on CD albums from a record store when you could get the songs you really wanted to hear for free on your computer? The CD bonanza of the 1990s quickly turned into the drought of the 2000s as sales of albums plummeted by more than 25 percent, from 785.1 million in 2000 to 588.2 million in 2006.[1]

The recording industry's strategic response to its sudden predicament was swift and predictable: Take legal action to shut down Napster and file copyright infringement lawsuits against more than 20,000 file sharers. Despite their success in executing their two-pronged legal strategy, the music executives failed to meet their prime objective of preserving the dominance of their longstanding business model. They won the battle but lost the war.

In the end, the golden goose was dead along with the thousands of record stores that no longer populate our shopping malls. In the heat of their legal battles to preserve the past, the managers of the recording industry failed to recognize that they had been suddenly thrust into a new world with a new set of rules. Had these managers recognized that their world had been turned permanently upside down, perhaps they would have bought Napster rather than put it out of business, and then maybe we would all be buying our digital downloads from the new Napster rather than from iTunes. The managers at Apple, unlike their counterparts at the record companies, were quite adept at the new rules, which explains how the computer company was able to become a major player in the music industry.

The recording industry is not alone in failing to recognize that we suddenly find ourselves in a completely new world with a completely different set of rules. Blockbuster, the king of video rentals, saw its business model disrupted twice—once by a disgruntled customer who hated late fees and responded by starting Netflix, and then again by the technology of on-demand video. By the time the managers at Blockbuster realized their world had drastically changed, it was too late for them. In 2010, they were forced into bankruptcy and eventually auctioned off to Dish Network in 2011.

In 2001, Borders was at the height of its popularity when online sales became a new way to purchase books. Although the brick-and-mortar business briefly considered developing an online capacity, the managers at Borders saw Internet book sales as a sideline at best and made the short-sighted decision to outsource their e-commerce to Amazon, a mistake that would prove fatal when Borders shuttered its doors in 2011.

Even supposedly "great" companies can fail to recognize when the world around them has suddenly changed. Circuit City and Fannie Mae, two of the eleven companies that met Jim Collins's rigorous criteria as "good-to-great" businesses, succumbed to the difficulties of managing in fast-changing times. In 2008, Fannie Mae found itself at the center of the storm in the worst financial crisis since the Great Depression, and in 2009, Circuit City collapsed into bankruptcy, falling victim to hubris and a se-ries of poor management decisions.

The struggles faced by each of these familiar companies are not iso-lated instances, but are rather reflections of a new and troubling norm. According to Nathan Furr in a 2011 blog post on Forbes.com, current trends indicate that the replacement rate for companies listed on the *Fortune* 1000 for the ten-year period ending in 2013 is very likely to be over 70 percent.[2] This is a dramatic increase from the period 1973–1983, when the replacement rate was only 35 percent.

Increasingly, as more companies and their managers are confronted by their own unprecedented challenges, many are beginning to come to terms with the unavoidable reality that the world most of them have known is indeed rapidly changing. As they continue to watch household brands they once considered invincible fall by the wayside, many of these managers are anxious about making sure their companies respond differ-ently. As unwelcome as the new reality may be, they are determined not to experience a similar fate.

GETTING ON THE RIGHT BUS

In their search for new solutions to effectively avoid the pitfalls of rapid change, a popular image that has connected with many managers is Jim Collins's notion of "getting the right people on the bus."[3] In his bestselling study of businesses that made the leap from good to great, Collins found that, unlike most companies' usual practice of figuring out what to do and then finding the people to do it, the leaders who guided these extraordinary organizations did the opposite. Collins discovered that "they *first* got the right people on the bus and *then* figured out where to drive it."[4] Given the increasing uncertainty and complexity in today's fast-moving markets, it is not surprising that perplexed executives would latch on to the notion that many of their problems would be solved if only they had the right people.

But what if having the right people is not enough? For most of their long lives, Blockbuster, Borders, Circuit City, and the various major players in the music industry were very well-managed businesses. Surely, getting the "right people on the bus" was not a problem for them. Perhaps their fatal flaws had less to do with the deficiencies of the people and more to do with the limitations of established management practices. Perhaps it wasn't the people on the bus, but rather the bus itself that was the problem. While "getting the right people on the bus" is important, isn't it just as important to be on the right bus? After all, you can gather all the right people you need and you can even determine the right direction that you need to take, but if you're on the wrong bus, you're not going to get where you need to be going. That's a problem when getting to where you need to be going is management's most important job.

The bus of business is management: It is the primary vehicle that businesses use to create products, coordinate operations, build market share, and remain profitable. Most businesses today continue to employ a management discipline that was initially formulated in the late nineteenth century and solidified in the early twentieth century by the first management guru, Frederick Winslow Taylor. Taylor developed the fundamental management model that guided the evolution of the modern corporation throughout the twentieth century. Known as Scientific Management, this model was designed to boost the efficiency and productivity of workers by applying scientific methods, such as time and motion studies, to discover the best ways for workers to perform the various tasks of production under the close supervision of a hierarchy of managers. Taylor's philosophy quickly became the gospel of management and provided the foundation for much of what many of us, more than a century later, still consider to be the givens of professional management: top-down hierarchies, the sharp divide between managers and workers, centralized decision making, and functional organization. Taylor's influence on the practice of management has been so pervasive and enduring that the late Peter Drucker referred to Scientific Management as "the one American philosophy that has swept the world—more so than the Constitution and the Federalist Papers."[5] This bus has indeed had a long ride.

THE UNPRECEDENTED COMBINATION

In these first decades of the twenty-first century, managers are beginning to come to terms with the reality that a nineteenth-century management model, despite its enduring success, is no longer adequate to address the challenges of a post-digital world. They suddenly find themselves in a different and unfamiliar world that's becoming more complex and chaotic as they painfully learn that the old rules no longer work. They are struggling to understand what's happening, why now, and—most importantly—what they can do about it.

With the advent of the Digital Revolution over the last decade, the way the world works has been radically transformed by the unprecedented combination of three developments: accelerating change, escalating complexity, and ubiquitous connectivity.

Accelerating Change

Let's look at the first of these developments, *accelerating change*. We now live in a fast-forward world where the speed of market evolution has overtaken every industry and dramatically altered the business landscape. That's why we call this new world the *wiki world*. As previously stated, *wiki* is the Hawaiian word for "quick" or "fast," and it aptly describes a business landscape where managing at the pace of change is becoming the central challenge. While most managers across all industries readily acknowledge that the world is moving faster, what they often fail to comprehend is that the increment of time for market change is now shorter than the increment of time for moving information up and down a chain of command. This means that the social structures of hierarchical organizations cannot keep pace with the speed of change in today's faster-moving markets. When you have to manage at the pace of accelerating change, organizations have to be built for *speed*.

Being built for speed means that organizations are highly adaptive to change. It means they are able to quickly respond to major market shifts with agility, flexibility, and imagination. These are not attributes that we normally associate with traditionally managed companies. Hierarchies are inherently slow, rigid, and incremental, and they are thus not designed to think boldly. Yet, when the speed of change becomes overwhelming, calculated boldness is often the only path to adaptability. Unfortunately, despite the numerous efforts at so-called change management initiatives, most organizations are changing at a much slower rate than the world around them, which explains why the recording industry managers preferred the incremental strategy of rigorous litigation to taking the bold leap into the new market of digital downloading. However, if managers want to succeed in the wiki world, learning how to be bold and adaptable is not an option—it's a strategic necessity.

Escalating Complexity

The second development that has transformed the world is *escalating complexity*. Today's business issues are substantively different from those of even a decade ago. For well over a hundred years, management issues have been mainly about solving problems, which explains why problem-solving skills have been so highly valued and why traditional management reveres individual experts and star performers. Industrial Age problems were, for the most part, issues of complication. Thus, when something went wrong, the challenge was to find the discrete elements among a myriad of details that, once corrected, would solve the whole issue. When the primary business challenges are issues of complication, star performers and their analytical tools are the pathways to uncovering the "silver bullets" that lead to problem resolution.

However, in the wiki world, our challenges are more likely to be issues of complexity where there are no silver bullets that neatly solve the problems. Issues of complexity are usually paradoxes where a balance needs to be struck between apparently contradictory perspectives or where problem resolution involves crafting a holistic solution that creatively integrates a collection of elements. Resolving paradoxes often requires the development of innovative cross-functional processes to uncover new ways of thinking and acting. The economic challenges that plague both the European nations and the United States are examples of complex issues in which the resolution continues to remain evasive because we lack the processes to effectively discover the common ground required for effective holistic solutions. As our issues grow increasingly more complex, organizations are learning that they cannot succeed unless they are built for *innovation*.

Innovation is the willingness to abandon what made success possible yesterday and the openness to create a very different future. It is the willingness to embrace the late Steve Jobs's bold counsel to "think different."

Innovation is the willingness to build a team, as Google does, to disrupt a very successful product offering so that when it is displaced in the market, it gives way to a new product that you produced rather than your competitor. It is the willingness to not be overly committed to one business model so that when it inevitably dies, the company naturally evolves into an adaptive strategy. Innovation is the willingness to develop a tolerance for failure and to learn how to embrace small failures, because that's the only way for organizations to avoid the big failures. And finally, innovation is the willingness to involve customers and workers as true partners in shaping the direction of the business because, in fast-changing times, the most important knowledge is often found outside the C-Suite.

Unfortunately, becoming innovative is a major challenge for most businesses because the old bus of management was not built for innovation. It was designed for discipline, predictability, enhancing the status quo, and preserving the authority of those who are in charge. As a consequence, most managers don't understand innovation and are significantly handicapped in markets that require creative thinking and nimble adaptability.

Too often, when traditional managers begin an innovation initiative, their first move is to set up a new department, put somebody in charge, and hold that person accountable for the new function. However, while well intentioned, these so-called innovation initiatives rarely produce real results. And in those instances where innovative managers do succeed, their accomplishments are typically short-lived because their innovative ways of thinking and acting are threatening to the more powerful custodians of traditional norms.

Innovation is not a department; it is the fuel of the new bus of management. It is a way of thinking and acting that values customers over bosses, collective intelligence over individual experts, shared understanding over top-down direction, simple rules over bureaucratic procedures, and transparency over control. Becoming innovative means altering the fundamental DNA of a business and its management so that creativity—which Jobs defined as the simple ability to connect things—becomes the fundamental fabric of the enterprise. Innovative companies are designed for serendipity and the daily cross-pollination of ideas because they understand that innovation isn't something that's planned and manipulated—it's something that's facilitated and emerges. That's why, as you will discover throughout this book, the social processes of innovative companies are inherently iterative and cross-functional.

Ubiquitous Connectivity

The third development transforming the world, *ubiquitous connectivity*, is the most important of the three because it is this element that makes the combination of the three developments unprecedented. There have been times in the past when we have experienced both accelerating change and escalating complexity, especially during the early stages of the Industrial Revolution. However, the sudden emergence of a hyper-connected world made possible by the Digital Revolution is truly unprecedented. We now live in a world where, for the first time in human history, we have the technology that makes mass collaboration possible, practical, and pervasive. Today, large numbers of geographically dispersed individuals can effectively and directly work together in real time—and they can do it faster, smarter, and cheaper than traditional businesses. That's why the best companies in our new wiki world are built for *collaboration*.

Mass collaboration is creating entirely new ways of working together that only twenty years ago would have stretched the limits of believability. Who would have imagined that you could build a successful computer operating system or an online encyclopedia using only volunteers working without a plan, without assigned tasks, and even without pay? Yet today, the open source Linux operating system is a $35 billion enterprise with a 12 percent market share, and Wikipedia has completely displaced a two-century-old business model in a single decade.

Mass collaboration can take many different forms. In addition to harnessing the individual contributions of a global corps of volunteers in open source communities, it can be a b-web where different independent companies, each retaining its own identity, come together in an Internet business alliance to leverage their strengths in a common platform. Mass collaboration can also be three geographically dispersed teams working together on a common project in shifts around the globe, giving new meaning to working 24/7. Or it can be a critical mass of managers and workers collaborating as a cross-functional team using creative meeting processes to identify breakthrough solutions to next-generation business problems. What all these forms of mass collaboration have in common is the capacity to expand an organization's intelligence and to increase its speed using sophisticated methods of collaboration in ways that challenge the conventional management wisdom of hierarchies.

As the Internet continues to flatten the world, the emerging capacity for mass collaboration will also flatten organizations and create new possibilities for business alliances as more companies discover that new ways of organizing large numbers of people are a competitive necessity if businesses are to take advantage of the remarkable speed and effectiveness of hyper-connected networks.

Today's new collaborative enterprises will create pressure for hierarchical companies to become more flexible and nimble if they hope to compete in the new economy of the wiki world. As it becomes more common for managers to be accountable for initiatives where they have no direct reporting relationship with many of the key staff on their project teams, managing by control will no longer be an option. When critical staff work for another company in the business alliance or work in another country on the other side of the globe, collaboration based on a shared understanding becomes a necessity for getting the job done, and this requires a substantial transformation in management skills and practices.

MOORE'S LAW

The unprecedented combination of accelerating change, escalating complexity, and ubiquitous connectivity is radically redefining the fundamental work of management. Of the three factors, the one that managers report feeling the most is accelerating change. For those managers who continue to follow the practices of a century-old management discipline, the pace of a fast-forward world and its constant demands to do increasingly more with less is nothing short of overwhelming. As they struggle to find their footing in the new landscape of the wiki world, many managers are seeking refuge in change management initiatives. Unfortunately, anecdotal evidence suggests that more than 75 percent of these initiatives fail. Perhaps that's because the very notion of change management is probably an oxymoron. To think that you can manage change is to imply that you can somehow control change. Change is going to happen whether we approve of it or not. Quite simply, change is impervious to our attempts to manage it. When it comes to change, the central challenge is not about managing change. It's about managing at the pace of change, and that is an entirely different proposition because the only way you can manage at the pace of change is to change how you manage. To understand why this is so, we need to understand a phenomenon that has come to be known as Moore's law.

In the mid-1960s, Intel cofounder Gordon Moore observed that the number of transistors that could be placed on a computer chip was doubling every twenty-four months. Said another way, our capacity to store and process information doubles every two years. Moore's law is the catalyst behind the unprecedented combination of change, complexity, and connectivity. It is also the force that has thrust us into the wiki world. Moore's law explains why today's average teenager has more computing power in her iPhone than the typical *Fortune* 500 company of the 1960s had in its multimillion-dollar computer center. It also explains why a nineteenth-century management model is unsustainable in a twenty-first-century world.

Figure 1-1 graphs Moore's law for the period 1984 through 2012. We begin with 1984 because that is the year Apple introduced the first Mac and transformed the computer from a piece of high-priced institutional equipment into an affordable household appliance available to the masses. We define our computing capacity in 1984 as one unit and then double that amount every two years. In 2012, our capacity to store and process information was more than 16,000 times what it was in 1984. To highlight how rapidly change, complexity, and connectivity will continue to reshape the business landscape, in 2014 that capacity will grow to more than 32,000 times when compared with 1984.

If a picture is worth a thousand words, this graph captures the dynamics of our journey between two very different worlds and serves as an analogy to explain where we have been, where we are going, and why what worked yesterday won't necessarily work tomorrow.

The first part of the graph, between 1984 and 2004, is essentially a flat, linear line. Using the graph as an example, if you were a manager in 1995

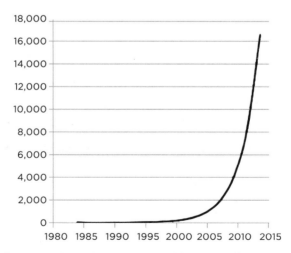

Figure 1-1. Capacity to store and process information.

and were responsible for planning and delivering specific business results for 1998, you would analyze all the available data at your disposal for the period 1990 through 1995. You would thoroughly study all the dynamics and the relationships among the key factors that would guide your decisions in planning for what you would need to do to meet your 1998 goals. With this knowledge, you would do what other successful managers had done for decades. You would forecast the future based on your thorough analysis of the past, and chances are highly likely that you would indeed deliver on the results because, on our graph, 1998 is a linear extrapolation of the period that precedes it.

For the past century, the way we've managed our businesses has been based upon two fundamental assumptions that have been rock solid for all that time. The first assumption is that the past is a proxy for the future. This explains why the professional practice of management has been so data driven. In a linear world, when management's job is to create the future, the secret sauce is to understand and then extrapolate from the past. The second assumption holds that the smartest organizations are those that leverage the intelligence of their smartest individuals. Accordingly, the dominant and near-universal structure for both private and public sector organizations has been the top-down hierarchy, where the few at the top direct the activities of the many, based on the belief that the whole organization becomes smarter than it would otherwise be if the workers were allowed to follow their own judgments.

Now let's examine the second part of the graph. If you were a manager in 2005, accountable for meeting specific business goals in 2008, and you built your business plans on the extrapolation of your analysis of the period 2000–2005, chances are highly likely that you would miss the mark because 2008 is not a linear extension of the period 2000–2005. That's because, beginning sometime around 2004, the line in the graph becomes exponential.

The significance of the graph of Moore's law is that it pictorially demonstrates that we have been rapidly and suddenly thrust into an exponential world in which the rules are very different. In our exponential world, many managers are painfully discovering that the past is no longer a proxy for the future, and they are reluctantly learning from the remarkable successes of innovative businesses—such as Google, Linux, and Wikipedia—that the smartest organizations are now the ones that know how to aggregate and leverage their collective intelligence by designing organizations not as top-down hierarchies but as powerful collaborative networks.

MANAGING THE FUTURE

With the rapid convergence of accelerating change, ubiquitous connectivity, and escalating complexity spawned by the transformational power of Moore's law, we have been suddenly thrust into a world where navigating the future can no longer be easily accomplished by scientifically extrapolating from the past. However, while the future may be very different—even radically different—from what we know today, it is not necessarily unmanageable. It just needs to be managed differently.

Managing the future no longer begins with a managerial elite setting the direction for the business; rather, the future today is more likely to start on the fringes of a hyper-connected world far from the control of those who think that they are still in charge. The management thought leader Gary Hamel correctly observes that, while the future may no longer be an extrapolation from the past, it is nevertheless often hidden in plain sight. Quoting the author William Gibson, Hamel counsels, "The future has already happened, it's just unequally distributed."[6] According to Hamel, companies miss the future not because it's unpredictable or unknowable, but because it's unpalatable and disconcerting. Nevertheless, if companies are to thrive in an exponential world, they are going to need to learn how to manage differently. Rather than leading functional silos, they will need to become comfortable at building well-connected agile teams that know how to change without trauma.

Unfortunately, most managers don't have much experience with exponential change. They are much more seasoned in the ways of discipline and efficiency shaped by a management ideology where control is the principal preoccupation. However, in times of accelerating change, it isn't the most controlled or the most efficient organizations that survive, but those that are the most adaptable and resilient. When exponential change supplants incremental change as the norm, the capacity to change without trauma becomes essential for the simple reason that the severe stress of never-ending crises is unsustainable for most human organizations.

The greatest impediments to building resilient organizations are the control systems that have served as the standard of management excellence for so long. Resilience requires innovation, exploration, experimentation, and—most of all—creativity. To be resilient, managers must have a capacity for iterative learning, which means that they must have a willingness to take risks, to sometimes fail, and to learn from small failures. While embracing explorative failure may be a hard adjustment for control-oriented managers, they may not have a choice because avoiding small failures in times of great change may turn out to be the fastest pathway to ultimate failure in a world where only the innovative survive.

One of the most significant consequences of the sudden emergence of the wiki world is a radical shift in the way that power works, especially in large organizations. At Google, Linux, Wikipedia, and many of the other companies we'll meet throughout this book, power comes not from being in charge but from being connected. As a result of this power shift, the most effective organizations are increasingly collaborative networks. These network-based organizations are far more adaptable and resilient than their traditional counterparts because they have proactively embraced a radically different management model—which we call Wiki Management—and as a result, they are better designed for managing the future because they are built for speed, innovation, and collaboration.

A BETTER WAY

The problem with using hierarchical management as a business strategy for handling wiki-world challenges is that the traditional management model is—by design—slow, incremental, and compartmentalized. Command-and-control structures are inherently bureaucratic and protective of the status quo, and as a result, they are poorly designed for managing at the pace of change, promoting innovation, or facilitating cross-functional collaboration. Nevertheless, many managers find themselves in the difficult position of recognizing that the world has indeed changed, yesterday's management wisdom has become today's management folly, and established methods and practices that had always delivered predictable results in the past aren't so reliable anymore. Yet, while these managers are ready to embrace new ways of thinking and acting, they are thwarted in their efforts for real change by the entrenched power dynamics of a C-Suite heavily invested in the belief that being in charge is more important than being connected. This creates a real conundrum for today's managers: How do you manage for speed, innovation, and collaboration when your organization is designed to remain slow, incremental, and compartmentalized?

In February 2001, seventeen software developers gathered in Snowbird, Utah, to pool their collective intelligence to formulate a strategy for effectively handling this conundrum. Among them were Jeff Sutherland and Ken Schwaber, the coauthors of what has come to be known as Scrum, and Ward Cunningham, the originator of the wiki, which became popularized with the explosive growth of Wikipedia. These software developers were convinced that there had to be a better way to do their work that would overcome the intrusive and unproductive constraints of traditional management practices. The result of their efforts was the crafting of the one-page Agile Manifesto and the birth of a management movement that, according to business author Stephen Denning, is "the best-kept management secret on the planet."[7]

The Agile Manifesto is a set of four management principles that outline a better way to align organizational work around speed, innovation, and collaboration. Agile management methodologies call for doing work in self-organized, cross-functional teams. These teams generally work in iterative phases lasting from two to four weeks, with clear deliverables at the end of each phase. The interim deliverables are assessed in facilitated collaboration sessions to make sure the work continues to meet customer expectations and to incorporate any changes that may have emerged during that phase.

In Agile software development, the role of the manager is radically transformed. Rather than being the overseer or controller who is directing and manipulating all aspects of project development, the manager's principal role is to coach the collective team and its individual members, to guide the group in reaching its own conclusions about the state of the project, and to facilitate effective discussions in the cross-functional collaboration sessions.

Since its inception in 2001, this management movement has produced extraordinary results in hundreds of companies around the globe under the labels *Scrum* and *Agile*. Nevertheless, the way Agile teams achieve their success has remained largely "under the radar" because software developers are often fairly isolated from the rest of their business colleagues, and engineers are not perceived as "real managers." In addition, even if their different ways of working are observed by traditional managers, they are quickly dismissed as idiosyncratic because they do not conform to the accepted ways of the so-called real managers.

For those managers who understand that they need to update their practices, there is a strong likelihood that within each of their companies, there is a group of people who are highly skilled in both the practices of a better way and in the political savvy to effectively propagate an effective management subculture. These practitioners of "the best-kept management secret on the planet" may be a powerful resource for managers who are serious about finding a better way. Several of the best practices of the Agile management community are outlined later in this book.

For more than fifty years, we have known that participative management is far superior to traditional legacy management. Beginning in the 1960s with Douglas McGregor's identification of Theory X and Theory Y and with Abraham Maslow's penetrating insights into the higher reaches of human nature, we have understood that when managers involve employees in defining the work to be done, the workers are more engaged in their efforts and more committed to performance. Unfortunately, this knowledge has had little real impact on organizations. While the interpersonal skills of managers have improved when compared with some of the Draconian practices of the mid-twentieth century, the involvement of workers has been limited to selective consultation. When it comes to implementing the insights of the human relations discipline spawned by McGregor and Maslow, management's accommodations have been far more about style than substance.

Regardless, substantive change is coming to management, and it's not coming from the insights of the psychologists or the organizational specialists, but rather from the innovative practices of engineers. The Agile Manifesto was written by software engineers. It was engineers who created the wiki and founded Google. And it was an engineer who, in 1958, created W.L. Gore & Associates, a company in which there are no supervisors and that has, over its fifty-plus years, made a profit in every year as it has grown to become a $3 billion business with 9,500 associates in thirty countries around the world. The psychologists and sociologists may have identified the right direction, but it's the engineers who have found a way to get on the right bus.

REBALANCING VALUES

In a recent global survey of more than 1,700 chief executive officers, researchers at IBM found that the CEOs identified empowering employees through values as an essential driver of high performance.[8] When we think of values, what usually comes to mind are virtues, such as integrity, honesty, fairness, and trust. These virtues are the attributes that are generally reflected in well-meaning corporate mission statements. Unfortunately, in far too many instances, these values are more "talk" than "walk." Despite management's best intentions, corporate mission statements rarely become corporate behavior templates. Why, if values are so important to performance, do so many organizations have trouble walking the talk? Perhaps it's because managers are focused on the wrong values.

Virtues are like blooming flowers. They are the most visible and the most defining part of a plant. But flowers are also the plant's most vulnerable part. Without solid roots, fertile soil, and plentiful water, flowers quickly shrivel and die. So it is with business organizations. Wherever we find organizations, such as Zappos and Google, that are blossoms of virtuous values, we also discover the fertile soil of a collaborative culture rooted in a subtle set of structural values.

An effective business organization is the intersection of three workable models: a business model, an operating model, and a management model. In defining these models, managers generally need to make a series of structural value choices among the five sets of paradoxical values presented in Figure 1-2.

Figure 1-2. Structural value choices.

Serendipity **vs.** Planning

Self-Organized **vs.** Centrally Organized

Emergent **vs.** Directed

Simple Rules **vs.** Detail Coordination

Transparency **vs.** Control

In approaching these choices, the best option is usually a balance between the two paradoxical values rather than a selection of one value and the dismissal of the other. To understand how these choices work, let's borrow an analogy from the field of psychology.

The late psychologist Erik Erikson developed a model of human development that postulated that every person moves through a progression of eight psychosocial stages to reach her full development.[9] The developmental task of each of these stages is the resolution of the tension between two paradoxical psychosocial values. So, for example, in the first stage—Basic Trust vs. Basic Mistrust—an individual needs to choose between these two values in approaching and dealing with other people. In the healthy personality, this is not an "either/or" choice but rather a "both/and" balance. While it may appear at first blush that trust is a virtue and the obvious choice in this paradoxical pair, keep in mind that a person who is always trusting is often regarded as a "Pollyanna." Similarly, one who is always mistrusting is considered to be paranoid. The healthy person develops a sense of both trust and mistrust, but not necessarily in equal parts. In striking a balance between the two values, the psychologically fit person has a clear preference for trust over mistrust. In other words, while she usually leads with trust, she is savvy enough to know when to mistrust.

The dynamics of this analogy apply to organizational development. As businesses move from the entrepreneurial stage to growth and then to maturity as large established companies, their leaders need to make a series of structural value choices. In resolving these paradoxical value choices, they need to strike a preferential balance of one value over the other.

Since their inception well over a century ago, corporations have clearly preferred the values shown on the right in Figure 1-2 over those on the left. Over time, these preferences have become so solidified that many, if not most, traditional organizations today find themselves in a position where they value only the items on the right to the exclusion of those on the left. This explains why the longstanding tasks of management have been defined as planning, organizing, directing, coordinating, and controlling. It also explains why in the typical top-down hierarchical organization, there are hardly any simple rules and little self-organization and transparency, and why serendipity and emergence are foreign concepts. This also explains why so many companies have difficulty in walking the talk when it comes to virtuous values. It's hard to be trusting when the dysfunctional dynamics of bureaucratic silos foster intense internal competition in a zero-sum game for resources and control.

Now, a new breed of business leaders who are making very different value choices are providing increasing evidence that the blossoms of virtuous values are possible only when nurtured in the soil of the structural values shown on the left in Figure 1-2. With the advent of the wiki world and its newfound capacity for mass collaboration, we are witnessing the rapid emergence of a radically different management model that definitively prefers the structural values on the left. This new model, Wiki Management, is the new bus of management. Wiki Management assumes that the most effective organizations are highly connected, self-organized networks that are designed to leverage the power of collective intelligence and achieve extraordinary results. In this new model, while the traditional management tasks are not dismissed out of hand, they are greatly diminished as the defining structural values of effective management.

Changing how we manage is not easy, given the pervasive presence of hierarchical management. For a long time, power was about being in charge, and hierarchies were the right bus for traversing the challenges of the complicated issues of the twentieth-century industrial world. Today, with the rapid rise of mass collaboration, power now comes from being connected, and networks are the right bus for navigating the complexities of the post-digital wiki world.

The challenges for managers have never been greater than they are today. While many managers understand that they have to change how they manage to meet unprecedented business issues and to leverage new opportunities, they often have to do so within the constraints of organizational structures that are changing far more slowly than the world around them. They know that this change gap is increasing and unsustainable, and they want to find ways within their power to do something about it. And most of all—rather than join the 70 percent of businesses that will fall by the wayside over the next decade—they care about their companies and their customers, and they want both to be around ten years from now.

This book describes the principles, processes, and practices of a new management model for any manager who is ready to do her part to get on the right bus. It is based, in part, on my own experiences leading a large business unit inside a larger traditional organization. We were successful in building a highly effective collaborative network inside a deeply entrenched hierarchy, and in the process, we turned around two decades of low growth and low performance to catapult the unit to extraordinary performance and the single greatest five-year growth period in its history.

The chapters that follow outline the substantive transformation of the roles and responsibilities of managers in the new wiki world and provide practical guidance to managers who are serious about changing how they manage. As you read on, you will discover a whole new world of management, where businesses are truly designed around what's most important to customers, where leaders are facilitators, and where workers are highly engaged in both strategy and execution. But before you can get on the right bus, you may need to let go of some deep-seated beliefs about how management works. To get the most out of the ride, you may have to let go of an old mindset.

CHAPTER SUMMARY: KEY POINTS

→ A nineteenth-century management model, despite its enduring success, is no longer adequate to address the challenges of a post-digital world.

→ With the advent of the Digital Revolution, the way the world works has been radically transformed by the unprecedented combination of accelerating change, escalating complexity, and ubiquitous connectivity.

→ Innovation is the willingness to develop a tolerance for failure and to learn how to embrace small failures because that's the only way for organizations to avoid the big failures.

→ Today, the smartest organizations are the ones that know how to aggregate and leverage their collective intelligence by designing organizations not as top-down hierarchies but as powerful collaborative networks.

→ While the future in fast-changing times may be radically different from what we know today, it is not necessarily unmanageable. It just needs to be managed differently.

2

Letting Go of an Old Mindset

n 1958, after a seventeen-year career at the DuPont Company, a middle-aged engineer named Bill Gore decided it was time to do something radically different. He left behind the security of a well-paying job with a world-renowned company to literally start a business in his basement. From the very beginning, Gore knew that he wanted his new business to be different, especially in the ways that the people communicated with each other. Gore had no interest in building another corporate hierarchy where people watched what they said for fear of drifting from the "corporate line." He wanted his new company to be a bazaar of innovation and a marketplace of creativity. To accomplish his dream, he knew he needed to build a network, not a hierarchy.

Gore's time at DuPont taught him that hierarchies inhibit the most important conversations and that their top-down power dynamics too often killed good ideas and kept bad ideas alive. Gore often said that in hierarchical organizations, "communication really happens in the carpool," meaning that the carpool was the only place where people felt free to talk with each other without worrying about the chain of command.[1] In his new company, Gore did not want any impediments to conversations because he understood that the free interchange of ideas was the soil of innovation. And so, Gore built what he called a lattice organization where there would be no traditional organization charts, no chains of command, and no predetermined channels of communication. Instead, work would be self-organized by teams, projects would be accepted rather than assigned, and people would be held accountable to the members of their teams. A peer review process, similar to that used in law firms, would determine individual compensation. Thus, the workers would be rewarded based on their contributions to team success and would have an incentive to commit to more rather than less work.[2]

Bill Gore's organizational approach was extraordinarily innovative for the 1950s. No other company at the time was using a networked-based management model to organize the work of large numbers of people, and we can be sure that few, if any, of Gore's management contemporaries would have given his company any chance of surviving. According to the management mindset of the mid-twentieth century, a lattice organizational model would have been perceived as a guaranteed formula for chaos and failure. After all, how would anything get done if there were no bosses?

As it turns out, a great deal can get done in network-based organizations. With its consistent appearance on *Fortune* magazine's annual list of the "Best Companies to Work For" and its enviable track record of more than fifty consecutive years of profitability, W.L. Gore & Associates, the makers of Gore-Tex and countless other innovative products, is living proof that there is a radically different alternative model that companies can use to organize large numbers of people into a sustainable, thriving, and highly adaptive business.

More than fifty years after its founding, there are still no organization charts at Gore, and all work continues to be accepted rather than assigned.

While Gore does have a CEO and a small number of designated leaders for its four divisions and its companywide support functions, such as human resources and information technology, these leaders don't assign work to anyone.[3] Nobody at Gore—not even the CEO—tells anyone what to do or how to do it. There are no vice presidents or supervisors; there are only associates. Some of the associates may serve as leaders from time to time, but another leader never assigns this role. If you want to lead a project at Gore, you have to recruit followers. In true self-organizing fashion, the followers determine the leaders, and the leaders remain in their roles as long as they continue to maintain the respect and support of their peers.

Moreover, the associates usually have a voice when it comes to selecting who will fill those few permanent leadership positions. Before Terri Kelly, the current CEO, was selected to replace the retiring Chuck Carroll, the board of directors polled a wide cross section of Gore associates and asked them whom they'd be willing to follow. "We weren't given a list of names—we were free to choose anyone in the company," Kelly recalls. "To my surprise, it was me."[4]

Gore's longstanding success in employing its lattice organizational approach is a valuable management asset in a new world where the Digital Revolution has suddenly made networks far smarter and faster than hierarchies. As the new technologies of the wiki world continue to spawn a new breed of companies, we are seeing increasing evidence that a well-designed organizational network is a far superior alternative to traditional management structures. And, in some instances, transforming businesses from hierarchies to networks may literally be a matter of survival. Nevertheless, embracing this radically different alternative may be very challenging for business leaders schooled in the traditional ways of management because it means they will first have to let go of an old and deeply entrenched mindset. They will have to change their fundamental beliefs about how management works.

THE POWER OF MINDSETS

Despite Gore's longstanding success, including adding more than 1,000 jobs and increasing its revenues by 20 percent during the recent Great Recession, few companies have adopted the Gore management model. The same is true when it comes to emulating Toyota's remarkable achievements. While many companies have incorporated the Japanese automaker's operational innovations, such as lean manufacturing, they remain largely unaware of what Toyota considers its greatest innovation—its radically different management model, known within the company as the Toyota Way. In addition, wildly successful management innovators, such as Google, Amazon, and Zappos, are barely noticed by anxious managers intently focused on preserving established business models in an ever-changing world. Why, when innovative leaders are achieving extraordinary performance in an increasingly complex world, do so many traditional managers maintain a blind eye to what is clearly in plain sight? To understand why so many have trouble seeing what seems to be so obvious, we need to first understand the power of a mindset.

Mindsets are our pathways to understanding how the world works and how we fit into the world. They integrate the common assumptions, values, and beliefs that shape the ways of thinking and acting among large groups of people. Mindsets are useful social tools for processing the uncertainty and the ambiguity of the world around us so that we may have a shared point of reference around which we can organize a shared reality. This shared reality becomes the context in which we develop the ideas, concepts, and perceptions that become the mental models for social and economic relationships. While these paradigms help us to cope with reality and to make sense of our world, their inherent assumptions, values, and beliefs can become so strongly held that we collectively become unaware that mindsets are also mental boundaries that limit and constrain our thinking.

The notions, perceptions, and understandings that we share in common shape what we collectively see and, equally important, what we collectively don't see. These mental boundaries are often reflected in our language. For example, in English, there is only one word for snow, while Eskimo languages have many different words to describe different types of the white stuff. For Eskimos, snow is a significant part of their daily lives, and so their language reflects that they are able to perceive what those of us in more temperate climates fail to see. This shows that what we see often depends upon what our mindset trains us to recognize. In other words, what you see is what you get. If an Eskimo were to ask a New Yorker what type of snow he sees, he might be puzzled and say snow is snow—that's it. To which the Eskimo would probably shake his head and think that, when it comes to snow, New Yorkers just don't get it! Whenever we find ourselves thinking, "They just don't get it," we are experiencing a difference of mindsets.

Mindsets are not forever. They are held only as long as the underlying assumptions, values, and beliefs work and continue to be shared. This is especially true as we move from one socioeconomic era to another. These large-scale social shifts always produce new and radically different mindsets because knowledge breakthroughs and their related new technologies invariably disrupt the generally accepted assumptions, values, and beliefs about the ways the world works.

Mindsets often are built upon a dominant social metaphor that is derived from a game-changing technology. These dominant metaphors become powerful social tools because they define the fundamental structures of our social relationships and become the foundation for formulating the rules of everyday life.

For example, throughout the 8,000 years of the Agrarian Age, the dominant metaphor was the land, reflecting the pervasiveness of the agricultural technologies of the time. The land was the locus of daily life, where the vast majority of people earned their living on farms that served as the centers of both their family and their work lives. The ways the world worked were radically disrupted with the dawn of the Industrial Revolution in the late nineteenth century, when the machine replaced the land as the dominant metaphor for a new mindset that quickly transformed the rules of everyday life.

As the new socioeconomic era took hold, people migrated from the farms to the factories in huge numbers, the domains of family life and work life became segregated, and the new technologies of mass production gave rise to the creation of large corporations, which in turn spawned the then new discipline of management. This new discipline reflected the emerging dominant metaphor, which explains why the typical organization chart resembles a mechanical schematic. It also explains why traditional managers are now blind to the dynamics of the new organizational structure of innovative management models.

Because the business pioneers of the wiki world don't assume that organizations work like machines, many of them are abandoning the long-standing practice of formal organization charts. This abandonment is nothing short of heresy for traditional managers who can't comprehend how a business could possibly operate without a hierarchy of supervisors.

The organization chart is the embodiment of the fundamental assumptions of management commonly shared, until recently, by successive generations of both managers and workers. For a long time, we have firmly believed that if anything is to get done, someone needs to be in charge. Command-and-control management assumes that an organization's intelligence fundamentally resides in a select number of star performers who are able to leverage their expertise through the power to direct and control the work of others.

For well over a hundred years, we have all shared a social lens that believed in the need for bosses, the power of individual intelligence, and the preeminence of specialized knowledge. Most of us continue to believe in the necessity of top-down organization charts because, whether we realize it or not, we operate from an unquestioned mindset that assumes that projects are best handled when we break them into discrete parts, divide the labor, and then reassemble the finished work under the direction of a central leader.

We believe in organization charts because most of us accept that that's just the way it is. But is it? The millennials don't presume so. To their way of thinking, bosses aren't all that necessary, heroes are overrated, and the hoarding of knowledge makes absolutely no sense. This is because the millennials are the first generation to come of age in the new wiki world and the first generation to embrace an entirely different social mindset from the many cohorts raised in the twentieth century.

The continuing Digital Revolution and its technologies of ubiquitous connectivity have spawned a new mindset, which assumes that power is derived from being connected rather than being in charge and that the smartest organizations leverage the collective intelligence of the many rather than the individual intelligence of a few. Accordingly, the dominant metaphor for our new age is shifting from the machine to the network.

The millennials don't relate to a hierarchical world where human activity is broken up into parts and then put back together again. For them, the world is, always has been, and always will be an interconnected network. This is why recent college graduates have difficulty fitting into hierarchical organizations and why they don't believe in organization charts. It's not that they're choosing not to adapt to the traditional ways of thinking and acting; rather, they don't adapt because, quite simply, they can't. There is nothing in their mental DNA that will allow them to buy into a mechanistic mindset, as did so many previous generations. The only social lens they have ever known is a mindset that sees the world as a network, not a machine. Unfortunately, many traditional managers remain in the firm grasp of an increasingly obsolete paradigm, which inhibits their ability to recognize that they are living in a new world with new rules. Unless these managers can learn to see their organizations as networks rather than as machines, they will likely become casualties in a world reshaped by a radically different mindset.

New mindsets are usually not immediately well received because those who have vested interests in the old mindset can be counted on to vigorously resist any challenge to their understanding of the world and their position in that world. Our ways of thinking and acting often define our identities. Thus, letting go of one's mindset can feel like losing one's sense of identity. No wonder new mindsets meet such resistance— those invested in the old mindset are defending a threat to their identities. This means that we can surely expect that those whose identities are fully connected to hierarchical bureaucracies will rigorously fight any attempts to explore the possibilities of self-organized working arrangements. Regardless, with the recent emergence of the wiki world and its newfound capacity for mass collaboration, we may not have a choice. None of us will be able to stop the rapid ascendance of a new mindset that will shape the thinking and the behavior of every new generation for the foreseeable future. Whether we like it or not, the paradigm shift is very real.

PARADIGM SHIFT

Like the boy who cries "Wolf!" the term *paradigm shift* has been so over-used that we've become numb to its meaning. For many, the phrase is nothing more than the latest jargon used by leaders whose actions rarely match their words. As tends to happen with jargon, the term has been so over-applied and misused that it has become trivialized; as a consequence, when a true paradigm shift happens, it often remains hidden in plain sight. This becomes particularly problematic for business continuity because these transformational events invariably disrupt established business models. This was a painful lesson the managers in the newspaper industry learned in the last decade when their failure to recognize that their businesses were in the grasp of a paradigm shift became an irrevocable competitive disadvantage.

In 1995, software engineer Craig Newmark created an e-mail distribution list to notify fellow software developers of social events in and around San Francisco. As a newcomer to the Bay Area, Newmark thought this list of fellow geeks might be a good way for him to quickly build a community of friends and contacts and escape the sense of isolation that often accompanies a move to a new town. While Newmark intended the list to be a vehicle to broadcast social gatherings, serendipity took the budding Internet community in a very different direction when the growing list of subscribers began using the mailing list for general advertising postings. In particular, people who were looking to fill jobs discovered that the list was a great way to connect with job seekers possessing the skills they needed. In early 1999, as the popularity of the powerful classified advertising tool began to explode, Newmark was able to quit his regular job and work full-time running a new company he called Craigslist. Over the next few years, what began as a tool for meeting people became the deadliest competitor the newspaper industry had ever encountered when one of the industry's primary revenue sources rapidly evaporated. A new business model for classified advertising had emerged and had completely disrupted the conventional way of doing business. Because its managers failed to recognize the paradigm shift, the reign of the newspapers as the kings of classified advertising was gone forever.

When a paradigm shift occurs on a large social scale, as is the case today, there is a period of time when both the fading and the emerging mindsets coexist. This coexistence is rarely smooth because large-scale paradigm shifts, by their nature, are highly disruptive. As a practical matter, this time of transition creates unique and unprecedented challenges for many managers because they find themselves caught between two worlds. On the one hand, because they work closely with younger workers who are fully versed in digital technology and its new ways of thinking and acting, managers intuitively grasp—even though they may not fully understand—that the world is rapidly changing. On the other hand, these managers must continue to please the corps of senior executives who remain fully invested in the old ways of a fading mindset.

The successful managers in today's transitioning times are those who know how to skillfully navigate between these two worlds. However, before these managers could accomplish this challenge, they first had to learn how wiki-world organizations work.

COMPLEX ADAPTIVE SYSTEMS

The wiki world is a hyper-connected global network where people can work directly and effectively with each other without having to go through a central organization. These working arrangements are highly efficient because their leaders don't assume that their organizations work like mechanical systems. Instead, they view human organizations as complex adaptive systems.

Melanie Mitchell, a leading expert in the field of complexity science (the study of systems that demonstrate nonlinear dynamics), defines a complex adaptive system as "a system in which large networks of components with no central control and simple rules of operation give rise to complex collective behavior, sophisticated information processing, and adaptation via learning or evolution."[5] Examples include flocks of birds, colonies of insects, the biosphere, the human brain, and—of course—the Internet.

Intelligence Resides in the Whole System

Complex adaptive systems share three common organizing principles. The first is that intelligence resides in the whole system. This means that, while different individuals may hold specific knowledge or differing interpretations of a common reality, no one individual is capable of processing all the information within the system. Self-organizing systems produce intelligence only when they have the capacity to process the diversity of knowledge that resides within the whole system. Thus, organizations are most intelligent when they have a rich diversity of perspectives and the means to access the collective intelligence derived from all the different points of view. This is in stark contrast to the conventional belief that the smartest organizations are those that identify the brightest among them and leverage their individual intelligence by giving them the power to define organizational thinking and to direct the activities of the many workers.

Gaining access to collective intelligence requires a sophisticated information processing capacity. All companies maintain the usual electronic information technology systems. But effective self-organization is possible only when businesses also have the ability to process the abundance of human intelligence distributed throughout their organizations. This means that companies need to integrate social networking technology into their organizational processes as well as to embrace innovative forms of face-to-face meeting technologies. In most hierarchical organizations, this human dimension of information processing is generally lacking. However, as more managers come to appreciate that businesses are essentially information processing networks, they will quickly learn that any company that cannot effectively process the full scale of its human intelligence is operating with a severe limitation. The management author Margaret Wheatley wisely observes that "the greater the ability to process information, the greater the level of intelligence."[6] And in the wiki world, intelligence is the distinguishing competitive advantage.

Simple Rules Guide Complex Collective Behavior

The second organizing principle of complex adaptive systems is that simple rules guide complex collective behavior. This most important premise is completely counterintuitive to conventional wisdom. We usually think that complex structures will work only if we have detailed blueprints or a comprehensive set of rules and regulations. While this is usually true for mechanical tasks, it is not the way biology works. In the organic world, the secret to the effective execution of complex tasks is that order is created by the collaborative application of a few simple rules rather than by compliance with a complex set of controls.

For example, in *The Wisdom of Crowds*, James Surowiecki describes how a flock of birds accomplishes its group journey by creating a well-ordered formation that emerges from each of the birds following a set of four rules: (1) stay as close to the middle as possible, (2) stay two to three body lengths away from your neighbor, (3) do not bump into another bird, and (4) if a hawk dives at you, get out of the way.[7] By following this simple set of rules, the flock is able to self-organize its journey, reach its destination, and handle any predators it encounters along the way. There's no need for a dominant leader directing the activities of the flock when collaborative focus around a simple set of rules does a better job.

The self-organized flight of birds is just one of nature's many examples of how complex orderly structures emerge from a few simple rules and cooperative autonomous interactions. The high-order functionality of these complex adaptive systems clearly demonstrates that consistent execution does not necessarily require elaborate control structures. There are often circumstances where consistency is better served through the collaborative actions of self-organizing independent agents following a simple set of rules. Thus, one of the distinguishing features of complex adaptive systems is that responsibility for control and coordination rests with each of the individuals rather than with one central executive.[8]

Order Emerges from the Interaction of Independent Individuals

The third principle of self-organizing systems is that order emerges from the interaction of independent individuals. In the natural world, there are no blueprints. Order is not preordained before the work begins, but rather emerges through an iterative process between the individuals and their environment. Because natural processes are evolutionary, we can't know the result until it occurs. This is completely contrary to all the conventional wisdom about the importance of detailed planning for the effective accomplishment of results. The notion that a large organization would approach an important initiative without a specific plan, and instead would let the results be defined by the interaction of the workers, is completely contrary to a hundred years of accepted management practice. But this notion is precisely the secret behind the incredible success of W.L. Gore & Associates.

By embracing a management paradigm that assumes that an organization is a complex adaptive system, Gore is continually able to leverage its collective intelligence to shape both its strategy and its execution. While its processes may appear messy and chaotic, the order that emerges from Gore's self-organized management approach has served as a solid foundation for more than fifty years of extraordinary performance.

WIKI MANAGEMENT

Over the past two decades, we have seen a sudden rise in the number of companies that are consciously focused on not building traditional bureaucratic hierarchies. These include Google, Craigslist, Wikipedia, Linux, Zappos, Amazon, Whole Foods, the software company Salesforce, the tomato processor Morning Star, the video game developer Valve, and the online T-shirt company Threadless. Each of these companies was built as a network from its inception and has no history of ever being a hierarchy.

While the vast majority of established companies have not embraced the paradigm shift, there are a handful of enlightened organizations that have been clearly ahead of their time in understanding the power of well-built networks. In addition to Gore and Toyota, which both embraced network-based management more than fifty years ago, Johnson & Johnson, Procter & Gamble, 3M, and IBM are examples of businesses that have had the capacity to evolve with the times.

Whether these innovative and highly successful enterprises are products of the Digital Revolution or have long histories, when we examine how their organizations work, we find that their leaders operate from a very different mindset than their traditional counterparts. Accordingly, they don't follow the established disciplines of a nineteenth-century management paradigm. Instead, they are reinventing management for the twenty-first century and propagating a new paradigm that is far better suited for the business challenges of a hyper-connected world. We call this new paradigm Wiki Management.

The principles and practices of Wiki Management reflect a radical departure from the traditional assumptions, beliefs, and values about how organizations work. That's because today's most innovative leaders understand that the world has been dramatically redefined by two ideas whose time has come.

The first of these ideas is: *When human organizations have the processes to leverage collective intelligence, nobody is smarter or faster than everybody.* We see this assumption reflected in the management practices of Google, Linux, and Wikipedia, each built upon the groundbreaking principle that the smartest organizations are those with the capacity to quickly access the wisdom of the crowd and the ability to leverage the resulting collective intelligence into a level of performance so extraordinary that it wrecks all our beliefs about the ways large groups get things done.

Google, in particular, is rewriting the rules for how we manage large enterprises. While its meteoric rise is often associated with the quality of its remarkable search engine, the real story behind Google's extraordinary success is its revolutionary capacity to organize collective intelligence into an efficient operating model. Unlike the organizational design in most traditional businesses, the methodology that Google uses to rank the Web's content is not built to amplify the intelligence of individual experts.

Instead, PageRank is a process that quickly collates the collective intelligence of the masses to guide the order of its search results. Given that Google is the preferred choice for more than two-thirds of Web surfers, it's clear that Google has leveraged its discovery that nobody is smarter or faster than everybody into a profitable business model. It's this discovery that is making so many traditional companies very nervous, and with good reason. Once the leaders at Google fully understand that search is an application and that aggregating collective intelligence is the game changer, they are likely to migrate their formidable skills and talents into unsuspecting complacent industries, creating innovative operating models that will displace longstanding business platforms in the next decade as quickly as they dethroned the popular search engines of the last decade.

While it may take a little time for business leaders to get comfortable with the assumption that nobody is smarter or faster than everybody, our growing familiarity with the Internet will make it a little easier to accept this first revolutionary concept. It's the second idea that will be much more troublesome because it goes against the grain of the most fundamental belief for how we organize the efforts of large numbers of people: *In the smartest and fastest organizations, leaders do not have the authority to issue orders or to expect compliance.* In other words, when organizations learn how to leverage collective intelligence, they don't need bosses to get things done.

Most of us cannot conceive of organizations without bosses. We believe that companies would quickly slide into chaos if someone were not in charge. However, Linux, Wikipedia, and Google are extraordinarily successful precisely because their leaders have very limited authority. Linus Torvalds of Linux and Jimmy Wales of Wikipedia don't give orders or make assignments in their open sourced operating platforms. The volunteers of Linux and Wikipedia decide where they'll devote their efforts and are responsible for organizing their own work. And Google arranges its organization to make it impossible for its leaders to behave like traditional bosses. With a sixty-to-one ratio of employees to supervisors and the workers having the right to self-direct 20 percent of their time, Google managers are forced to learn new ways of leading where the ability to get things done comes from the power to connect and collaborate rather than the authority to be in charge and in control.

This second idea is so troublesome because it revolutionizes the practice of management, especially in large organizations. For more than a century, managers have been bosses, and the authority to issue orders and to expect compliance has been their defining attribute. While some have been more participative and others have been more autocratic, everyone inside a traditional organization understands that, regardless of style, the boss is in charge. However, as more businesses discover that their survival depends on their capacity to leverage collective intelligence, they will quickly realize that their continued reliance on a cadre of supervisors is the greatest impediment to meeting the new demands for innovation and speed in fast-moving markets. When nobody is smarter or faster than everybody, you don't need bosses editing or overruling collective wisdom.

However, diminishing the bosses does not mean that organizations do not need managers. In fact, in the new economy of the emerging Digital Age, managers are more important than ever. That's because collective intelligence needs to be processed and aggregated. Someone needs to guide the creation of our common ground and the shaping of our shared understanding, whether through electronic learning platforms, such as PageRank, or through large group collaboration sessions, such as the Open Space meetings that will be described in Chapter 6.

The managers who follow the disciplines of Wiki Management exert a different type of influence from their traditional counterparts. Rather than acting as controllers who take charge and make the decisions, they assume the roles of facilitators of the discovery processes from which the best decisions emerge. Thus, we are learning that the key to successfully managing in fast-changing times is to focus more on *making discoveries* and less on *making decisions*. That's because when you make the right discoveries, the right decisions are likely to follow. If businesses want to make sure that their organizations are designed for innovation, they can't let decision makers short-circuit the discoveries resident in their collective intelligence.

These two ideas, that nobody is smarter or faster than everybody and organizations don't need bosses to get things done, are the foundational assumptions of the new paradigm that is revolutionizing the practice of management. There's a reason that these two ideas are emerging now, and it has more to do with the times than it does the ideas. These two assumptions could never take hold in a world where hierarchies and mechanistic models continued to define our social organizations. The fact that these ideas have begun to take hold now is clear evidence that the business world we have known for the last 150 years is inevitably fading away. We are rapidly exiting the Industrial Age and entering the new and very different Digital Age. The defining characteristic of this new age is that its breakthrough technologies have indeed made networks far more powerful than hierarchies. That's why facilitative leaders leveraging collective intelligence by following the principles and practices of Wiki Management are increasingly outperforming traditional bosses who lack the wherewithal to let go of an old mindset.

FROM CONTROLS TO CONTROL

Letting go of an old mindset, embracing unfamiliar assumptions, and changing core beliefs take an enormous amount of courage. Adopting the three organizing principles of complex adaptive systems as the foundation for building a management discipline is counterintuitive, incredibly uncomfortable, and just plain scary for managers with long histories of leading by control. I can attest to this from personal experience. My own transformation from traditional management to Wiki Management happened when I was suddenly given responsibility for a large business operation that needed quick improvement. As I surveyed the business and assessed what was working and not working, I quickly came to the conclusion that the primary root of the operational problems was the misplaced use of a hierarchical management model in a complex business alliance. I wasn't sure exactly what we needed to do differently, but I knew we had to make a dramatic change, and I knew for certain that the continued use of a vertical management model in a horizontal business alliance was a guaranteed formula for failure.

Thus began a very personal business journey, where I discovered that, in fast-changing times, managing by control is an illusion and the only way to drive consistency in a knowledge economy is to have the ability to quickly build a broad-based shared understanding among the network of business partners. However, this was not as easy as it sounds, especially in the beginning. Before I could grow comfortable with using shared understanding to drive results across a network, I first had to learn how to give up control. And that was hard in a business with a multitude of details. While it may be an illusion, there is a deeply shared belief among managers that strong control is the only way to stay on top of complex details.

To continue to maintain a belief in managing by control is to ignore the reality that the current volume of details in large organizations today is already beyond the capacities of traditional systems of central control. The only way for large organizations to avoid drowning in an ever-expanding ocean of details is to cultivate a common perspective across all the managers and workers so companies are able to tap into and leverage their collective intelligence in real time. As the details of wiki-world businesses become seemingly infinite, businesses will be required to have competent processes for quickly and intelligently sorting through complexity, interpreting reality, and identifying the simple drivers of market success. These few drivers become the simple rules that allow large companies to behave as complex adaptive systems and successfully navigate the vast ocean of business details. While it may seem counterintuitive, simple rules actually do create a much higher order of control than the elaborate collections of controls so typical of the command-and-control organization.

Peter Drucker makes the point that we should not confuse the words *controls* and *control* because they have entirely different meanings.[9] Drucker notes that controls are analytical and provide information about past events, whereas control is normative and focused on future direction. This is an important distinction because, when the world is stable, the past can serve as a proxy for the future, and, therefore, systems of intricate controls can provide reliable assurances about the state of organizational control. However, in fast-changing times, the future is likely to be very different from the past, and systems of controls can actually weaken the overall state of control when change and adaptation are critical to future market success. In that case, control is better served by a clear focus on what's most important, which is reflected in a simple shared understanding that permeates the organization and helps to drive consistent and responsive adaptation to changing circumstances. The texture of control in complex adaptive systems is fundamentally different from the fabric of practice in mechanical systems.

FROM CONTENT TO CONTEXT

Management's primary focus has been and will continue to be the future. This is not going to change. What is changing is that, when the past is no longer a proxy for the future, managers have to stop monitoring the myriad of details as their primary strategy for fostering control in the organization. The details should be left to the people who are closest to the customers and more familiar with the business processes, and are thus also in the best position to execute quick and intelligent responses to changing conditions.

It's an uncomfortable yet true paradox of the new management paradigm: The most effective way for managers to ensure that their organizations remain under control is to give up the illusion that they can exercise personal control over the details of the work. That's because, in a network, the manager's primary focus is more on the context than the content of the work. This is the essential insight that guided Bill Gore as he built his lattice organization and Linus Torvalds and Jimmy Wales as they designed the open source platforms Linux and Wikipedia. Create the right context in which the work happens and the content takes care of itself. This is a difficult pill to swallow for leaders schooled in the traditional ways of managing, because they stubbornly hold on to an old mindset, believing their organizations would fall into a permanent state of chaos without their steady hands controlling the levers of the business.

Managing context requires a different set of competencies and a higher level of emotional intelligence than are needed to manage content. It's relatively easy to give orders and to require people to do things according to your way of thinking, especially when you have the power to withhold raises or even fire workers if they don't comply. It's more challenging to have the ability to quickly access collective thinking, to build shared understanding, and then to trust people's self-organization to get the job done. It's much easier to be convinced of your own intelligence and to impose your point of view on others than it is to trust the collective intelligence of the group or to detach yourself from your own opinions while you facilitate a consensus point of view. And it's more comfortable to believe in the illusion that a single intelligent and talented individual can lead an organization to greatness than it is to accept the reality that nobody is smarter than everybody and that the great leaders in our new wiki world are those who have the capacity to aggregate and leverage collective intelligence.

Organizations that want to master the challenges created by the unprecedented combination of accelerating change, escalating complexity, and ubiquitous connectivity can't afford the hindrances of the egos of so-called heroic leaders. They cannot allow a good idea to be stopped by a single boss, or the value of a suggestion to be weighted by the position of the speaker, nor can they tolerate a glacial bureaucracy that fails to meet evolving customer expectations or is too slow to recognize when customer values have suddenly shifted.

THE FIVE DISCIPLINES

The management architecture necessary to lead the networks of mass collaboration is very different from the organizational structure that successfully leveraged the machines of mass production. This difference is a reflection of a rebalancing of the fundamental structural values used to guide the ways of thinking and acting in day-to-day organizational life. In Chapter 1, we discussed how, in defining their business and management models, business leaders need to make a series of choices among five pairs of paradoxical values. We also observed that, for the past 150 years, the vast majority of companies have favored the values consistently taught in Business 101: planning, organizing, directing, coordinating, and controlling. And, until recently, those foundational disciplines have been unquestioned.

The new breed of managers leading the paradigm shift are making very different architectural choices in building their organizations by favoring the structural values of serendipity, self-organization, emergence, simple rules, and transparency. Accordingly, these practitioners of Business 2.0 are redefining the fundamental disciplines of management. When we closely examine the organizational behavior of the companies that are practicing Wiki Management, we discover that these enterprises are built around five very different disciplines that are rarely, if ever, practiced in traditional businesses. These five disciplines are:

1. Understand What's Most Important to Customers. In a hyperconnected world, the best companies are customer-centric. Their people clearly understand that they work for the customers, not the bosses. Accordingly, they build their strategies around what matters most to customers and design their processes to give *delighting customers priority over pleasing bosses*.

2. Aggregate and Leverage Collective Intelligence. In a knowledge economy, organizations are fundamentally intelligence systems. Today's most intelligent organizational leaders no longer leverage individual intelligence by constructing functional bureaucracies; rather, they cultivate collaborative communities with the capacity to quickly aggregate and leverage their collective intelligence. These enlightened leaders fully understand that nobody is smarter and faster than everybody, and as they build their organizations, they show a clear design preference for *building networks rather than hierarchies*.

3. Build Shared Understanding by Bringing Everyone Together in Open Conversations. Companies that successfully manage at the pace of accelerating change understand that the most powerful organizations are those that have the ability to gather the whole system in one place. By bringing everybody together and creating innovative processes to expand the conversations and effectively integrate diverse points of view, they have the rare ability to cocreate a powerful shared understanding that drives clarity of purpose across an entire organization. As the pace of change continues to accelerate, managers are increasingly discovering that *shared understanding is far more effective than compliance* in fostering organizational excellence.

4. Focus on the Critical Few Performance Drivers. The most effective leaders know that management is about creating the future. And when they are good at creating the future, they never have to explain the past. That's why smart leaders don't focus on outcome measures; they focus on the driver measures that create the outcomes. If you want to manage at the speed of change, *it's far better to lead than to lag*.

5. Hold People Accountable to Their Peers. The secret to mastering the unprecedented challenges of the wiki world is to make sure that no one in the organization has the authority to kill a good idea or keep a bad idea alive. In the best businesses, leaders aren't bosses; they're catalysts and facilitators orchestrating collaborative networks. The leaders of these networks consistently achieve extraordinary results because they understand that *holding people accountable to their peers rather than to supervisors* is the great enabler of the collaboration necessary for speed and innovation.

In addition to rebalancing structural values and redefining basic disciplines, embracing the new management architecture requires a reengineering of the fundamental relationships within the organization. In order to align organizational behavior with the choices made among the five pairs of structural values discussed in Chapter 1, managers need to make a similar series of choices among the five sets of relationship values presented in Figure 2-1.

Accordingly, if the balance of structural value choices favors serendipity over planning, self-organization over central organization, emergence over directed, simple rules over detail coordination, and transparency over control, the aligned balance of relationship value choices would favor customers over bosses, networks over hierarchies, shared understanding over

Figure 2-1. Relationship value choices.

Customers **vs.** Bosses

Networks **vs.** Hierarchies

Shared Understanding **vs.** Compliance

Leading **vs.** Lagging

Peers **vs.** Supervisors

compliance, leading over lagging, and accountability to peers over accountability to supervisors. Without the proper alignment of the relationship systems of the organization, the desired structural values and management discipline remain nothing more than wishful thinking, which explains why so many companies have difficulty walking the talk. The ways we structure the fundamental relationships in organizations is what drives the walk.

Letting go of the old management mindset is about recognizing that the fundamental work of management is no longer the traditional tasks of planning, organizing, directing, coordinating, and controlling. In the wiki world, the most successful managers focus their attention on the five disciplines outlined above. In the new management paradigm, the traditional management tasks are now performed by the self-organized workers who are much closer to the customers and the business processes, and, thus, are better able to quickly respond to fast-moving changes and increased customer demands. Later, we will explore the structural and relationship value choices and each of the five disciplines of Wiki Management in greater detail, and we will provide practical examples of how innovative managers are using the values and the disciplines of this new paradigm to master the unique challenges of our unprecedented times.

CHAPTER SUMMARY: KEY POINTS

→ Unless managers can learn to see their organizations as networks rather than as machines, they will likely become casualties in a world reshaped by a radically different mindset.

→ When a paradigm shift occurs on a large social scale, as is the case today, there is a period of time when both the fading and the emerging mindsets coexist. The successful managers in today's transitioning times are those who know how to skillfully navigate between the two mindsets.

→ One of the distinguishing features of complex adaptive systems is that responsibility for control and coordination rests with each of the individuals rather than with one central executive.

→ When human organizations have the processes to leverage collective intelligence, nobody is smarter or faster than everybody.

→ In the smartest and fastest organizations, leaders do not have the authority to issue orders or to expect compliance.

3

Resetting the 3 M's

n 1998, the last thing that the world needed was another search engine. After a short period of intense competition among a crowded field of upstarts, Yahoo's Web directory appeared to be on the verge of breaking away from the pack and establishing itself as the Web surfer's first choice for searching the Internet. Using a horde of expert editors, Yahoo had organized the myriad of Web pages into an impressive practical catalog. When surfing the Web, most people were finding their way to Yahoo because Yahoo's cataloging experts were better than those of their competitors.

However, cataloging takes time, and by 1998 the popularity of the Internet had begun to explode. The prodigious effort to keep up with the rapidly growing number of Web pages was becoming a challenge for even the best of editorial experts. It was at this time that Sergey Brin and Larry Page, two innovative entrepreneurs who had met as students at Stanford University, came up with the idea for a more effective and efficient way to catalog Web pages that would not require the use of experts. They created a sophisticated learning platform, which they called PageRank, that would rely on the collective knowledge of all the Internet users to catalog and rank Web pages. Thus, Google was born.

PageRank is an algorithm that lets users decide which Web pages are most relevant to a search based on the number of links and visits to a particular site. By tracking user search patterns and trends, Google's decentralized learning platform did a better job of quickly finding the right pages than Yahoo's centralized expert editors. It wasn't very long before Google's learning platform easily supplanted Yahoo as the search engine of choice.

Although Yahoo is an Internet company, its business model was shaped according to the mechanistic paradigm so prevalent at the time, and thus, the work of cataloging Web pages was seen as a planning and organizing task to bring order to complexity using the authoritative knowledge of experts. Brin and Page, however, operating from a very different paradigm, saw the work effort as a learning and collaborating task to discern the collective intelligence among all the Web surfers. In building their highly successful search engine, Brin and Page employed one of the basic principles of Wiki Management: Networks are smarter and faster than hierarchies. This principle has also served as the foundation for the innovative management approach that's made Google a perennial presence on *Fortune*'s list of the "Best Companies to Work For."

While Google is clearly recognized as a technological leader, the full extent of the company's influence has been underestimated because most of us have a very limited view of technology. When we think of technology, we tend to think of tools and gadgets. We marvel at the amazing breakthroughs in electronics and robotics. What comes to mind is the progressive stream of inventions over thousands of years from the very first wheel to the latest iPhone. For most of us, technology is about things. It's about the modern machines that make life easier, faster, and more convenient. However, there is another dimension of technology—one that is often overlooked because it has nothing to do with things. This other dimension is about people and the ways that people work together, and it is here that Google may be making its most important technological contributions. As we will learn in later chapters, Google's innovations in organizing the work of large numbers of people may be even more valuable than its methodologies for managing big data.

AN INEVITABLE REVOLUTION

The history of technology is an iterative journey. It's a journey between people and their things and between developments in physical technology and advances in social technology. There are milestones on this journey that mark the breakthrough moments when great leaps in physical technology dramatically reshape social technology. These landmarks proclaim the revolutionary transitions between the socioeconomic eras that shape our day-to-day experience and form our social mindsets. And so, throughout the history of civilization, these occasions have marked our passage from the Stone Age to the Agrarian Age, and then to the Industrial Age.

As our iterative journey continues, most of us are well aware that, with the convergence of personal computers, the World Wide Web, and fiber optics, we are witnessing a significant revolution in physical technology. However, very few of us realize that we are also at one of those rare historical milestones where a great leap in physical technology generates an inevitable revolution in social technology. Whether we realize it or not, today's emerging Digital Age is dramatically reshaping the work we do and the way we work.

It is difficult for us to comprehend just how quickly and how thoroughly the world of work is about to change. Nevertheless, we are at a tipping point in the evolution of large business organizations, where traditional corporations and their managers now find themselves in an unprecedented business reality for which they are almost totally unprepared. The signs are all around us, but we miss them because we continue to see the world through the social lens of an obsolete management paradigm that is rapidly losing relevance.

When we think of technology, we usually focus on physical technology because, over the last 100 years, that's where we have seen countless incremental changes. We have come a long way from the Model T Ford to the Toyota Prius and from rotary "party line" telephones to wireless cell phones. The history of the twentieth century was about the steady stream of inventions and progressive improvements in machines and their ability to make our lives easier and more convenient. If you've ever visited the Carousel of Progress at Disney World, you have a sense of all the improvements in lifestyle and quality of life brought about by the continual enhancements in physical technology throughout the last century.

Remarkably, however, we have seen little incremental change in our social technology. For more than a century, the social technology of work, especially in large organizations, has remained essentially unchanged. The hierarchical management model that was used to run the first large assembly lines is still used today to manage twenty-first-century organizations.

Some of you may protest, "That's not true! What about participative management?" Unfortunately, while the luminaries of worker involvement did indeed spark a human relations movement in the later part of the twentieth century, to be candid, their influence on management practices has been superficial at best. Sure, managers today are more benevolent when compared with the Draconian habits of the early Industrial Age bosses. However, when it comes to implementing the insights of the human relations movement, management's efforts have been far more about style than substance. Today's managers may spend more time soliciting input from their workers, but at the end of the day, the basic social technology remains the same: The managers are still the bosses, the workers are still subordinates, and the latter are still expected to do as they are told.

It turns out that while business leaders have been very willing to adjust the style of management to accommodate prevailing social trends, they have been most unwilling to modify the organizational structures that reinforce the manager's authority to assign work and to ensure workers' compliance with management's directives. However, the lip service paid to the values of participative management over the last half of the twentieth century may not be sustainable in our twenty-first-century world because, thanks to companies like Google, we now have access to both the physical and the social technologies that make networks far smarter and faster than hierarchies.

MANAGING INNOVATION

Managing innovation is now a critical core competency for businesses across all industries. That's because the key to managing at the speed of change is having the ability to continually innovate. Whereas in the past innovations tended to be more incremental and happened at a more measured pace, today innovation is more constant and clearly more disruptive. While it has always been true that every business model eventually becomes obsolete, what's different about today is how the accelerating pace of change is dramatically shortening the life span of business models. For example, in the mobile phone industry, we have had four different market leaders across the last four decades.[1] In the 1980s, Motorola invented the cell phone with its brick-shaped DynaTAC phone. The Finnish company Nokia reengineered the product in the 1990s by building a much smaller, easy-to-hold version of the product. In the first decade of the twenty-first century, the Canadian company Research in Motion dazzled the market with the BlackBerry, which became a big hit with businesses by integrating e-mail and telephone into one device. And then, in 2007, Apple completely disrupted and redefined the market with the iPhone, creating a complete telecommunications portal in the palm of your hand. While each of these four companies created a powerful innovation and quickly became market leaders, with the exception of Apple, none had the where-withal to move from one innovation to another. The difference between being innovative and managing innovation is that, while any new entrant can be innovative by creating the next new thing, skillfully managing in-novation is about moving from innovation to innovation. It's about dis-rupting your own business models because, if someone is going to displace your latest leading product, it might as well be you rather than a competitor.

One of the reasons networks are so smart and fast is that they are bet-ter designed for innovation. Building organizations as networks rather than hierarchies is a better strategy for moving from innovation to innova-tion. Because networks don't rely on strong centralized leaders, no one can silence the agents of new ways of thinking. In a fast-changing world where technology strongly favors the networks, hierarchies are at a clear disad-vantage when it comes to innovation.

Innovating in a hierarchy is like running on a treadmill. You expend a lot of energy. You work really hard. You seem to cover a lot of distance, but at the end of the run, you've moved nowhere. Despite all that effort, you're still at the same place you started. Top-down structures don't innovate well because too many managers have the authority to kill good ideas and keep bad ideas alive, too many meetings are endless debates that resolve very little, and too many of the measures that we use to compensate man-agers and workers are misaligned with delivering customer value.

RESETTING THE 3 M'S

If traditional managers want to step off the management treadmill and keep pace with fast-changing markets, they need to embrace the manage-ment paradigm shift by completely resetting their organizational principles, processes, and practices in three critical areas. We call this transformation resetting the 3 M's: resetting the managers, resetting the meetings, and re-setting the measures.

Managers, meetings, and measures are the three dimensions of day-to-day organizational life. Whether we are passionate about the place we work or we dread going to the office is usually related to our experience in these three dimensions. We can be sure that most of the people who work in the companies on *Fortune*'s list of the "Best Companies to Work For" feel their managers involve them in shaping the work, participate in meetings where learning happens and value is created, and understand how their performance measures connect with delivering what's most important to customers. On the other hand, there is ample anecdotal evidence that people in traditional companies are becoming increasingly frustrated by managers who don't listen, meetings that don't accomplish anything, and measures that don't make any sense.

Resetting the 3 M's is a radical transformation of the basic dimensions of management. Resetting the managers is primarily focused on *eliminating the sovereignty of the supervisor* by transitioning the leader's role from being the boss to being the facilitator. It means accepting the new reality that the power to be connected is now greater than the power to be in charge. Resetting the meetings is about *getting the whole system in one space* and transforming business gatherings from ineffective political debating jousts to powerful channels of collective learning by including more people in open conversations. And resetting the measures involves *measuring for collaboration* and putting in place performance systems that naturally encourage workers to work effectively together in serving the needs of the customers. This is accomplished by replacing disjointed metrics practices with a focused measurement discipline that collectively identifies the most important drivers of success and aligns key cross-functional goals with the delivery of customer value. When these resets are fully implemented, they are more than a cultural change: They are a radical transformation of the structural elements that create, and more importantly sustain, organizational cultures that continually achieve extraordinary performance.

Resetting the Managers

Since its inception, the key role in the command-and-control organization has been the boss. Based on the military model, bosses are arrayed into a hierarchy with supervisors reporting to managers who, in turn, report to officers, with everyone ultimately under the authority of the chief executive officer. These bosses issue directives, and their subordinates are expected to carry out those commands. Authority, flowing down from the top of the organization, ensures the orderly transfer of strategic objectives formulated by senior executives into tactical activities performed by the workers. Compliance with supervisory directives is a basic expectation and is continually reinforced through the performance appraisal process.

The fundamental structure of bureaucratic hierarchies reflects the core belief that, at every level of the organization, somebody has to be in charge with clear unquestioned authority or the organization risks falling into chaos. That's why everyone in a traditional company has a boss and why the fundamental role of the manager is to be a boss.

Another belief that permeates many traditional organizations is the notion that the most effective managers are usually the smartest people in the room. When these managers exert their will throughout the organization, what they are directing workers to do will be good for the company. Over time, this notion has shaped the profile of what we look for when hiring managers: smart, confident, take-charge individuals who can effectively persuade people to their way of thinking. This profile has long served as the backdrop for executive recruiting in both the private and the public sectors.

The first step in making the transition from leading hierarchies to leading networks is to reset the role of the managers. In networks, the most effective leaders are facilitators, not bosses. Given today's accelerated pace of change, heroes and stars attempting to centrally direct the work of large numbers of people are no match for self-organizing teams of knowledge workers who can work faster, smarter, and less expensively thanks to the new tools of the Digital Revolution. If companies want to succeed in the wiki world, they need to abandon the long accepted notion that a single intelligent and talented individual can lead organizations to greatness, and they have to divest their managers of their traditional authority to issue orders and to expect compliance.

Today, the central challenge of organizing large numbers of workers is about leveraging networks, accessing collective knowledge, and realizing the efficiencies of mass collaboration. This means that collective learning and self-organized work replace central planning and top-down directives as the foundation for effective strategy and execution. But more important, it means that the role of the business leader is no longer to act as a boss. Wiki Management leaders don't issue orders or expect compliance. Instead, they see themselves as responsible for managing the architecture for mass collaboration by creating collective learning processes, building quick consensus, cultivating shared understanding, and keeping the company focused on the few drivers that guide self-organizing teams of workers to consistently deliver customer value in fast-changing markets. In the new management paradigm, the true measure of a leader has more to do with mobilizing human capacity than with motivating individuals.

When the market dictates that the most effective leaders are facilitators, organizations have to be diligent in removing executive ego from the practice of management. That's why adopting Wiki Management inevitably leads to eliminating the long established sovereignty of the supervisor. There is no room for the command performances of heroic leaders or star performers when the system is the star and the workers are the true heroes of mass collaboration. In the networked organization, the central role is the knowledge worker and not the boss. The Digital Age is changing the work we do and the way we work, and—as we'll see when we discuss the specific practices of Wiki Management in later chapters—perhaps no group of people will feel this more than the current corps of managers.

Resetting the Meetings

The primary vehicle of managerial work is conversation. Whether they are in one-on-one discussions or in larger group gatherings, people in organizations spend much of their time moving from conversation to conversation in different types of meetings. Unfortunately, in most organizations, there is probably no more dysfunctional activity than the typical meeting. When managers are focused on control and compliance, conversations can quickly become monologues or debates, with little real interest in hearing what others have to say. By design, the structure and practices of the typical meeting in command-and-control companies drive and enable limited thinking.

The traditional meeting follows the committee format where the leader sits at the head of the table, individuals follow the cues of their superiors in bringing forward ideas, and what needs to be discussed often isn't talked about, as straight talk takes a backseat to political correctness. When managers are riveted on maintaining control, communication is a one-way street designed to get everyone on board with top management thinking.

Committee-style meetings are essentially controlled events where voices are stratified by position or function and all the voices are not equal. The opinions of the senior executives and the functional experts count more. Thus, they speak more often and more forcefully in forums where defending one's position and preserving the accepted ways have more value than exploring the novel notion or facilitating an inclusive dialogue. In a business world where the future is changing almost daily, most corporate meetings are nothing more than formal rituals to preserve yesterday's order, where bosses set the agenda, decide who has a need to know, and carefully script the conversations in closed gatherings where they make certain that everyone is clear about what is speakable and what is not speakable. And they make most inexpressible the very fact that some issues are inexpressible.

The ritualistic norms of the committee-style meeting are so well established that most participants are unaware that they engage in conversational practices that dismiss the opinions of others and shut down any opportunity to explore new directions. Even managers who consider themselves more enlightened participative leaders fall prey to the well-established norms if the only gathering format is the committee-style meeting. While these leaders may encourage everyone to speak her mind and make sure that everyone is heard, if the meeting itself is not a vehicle for integrating thinking and creating collective knowledge, then all you have is a polite respect for different opinions. Nothing really changes because the same people continue to control the same levers of power and authority when everyone leaves the room.

While making it safe for everyone to express her opinion is an important first step in opening up corporate conversations, it's not enough. In fact, it may actually do more harm than good by fostering cynicism if the expectations that things will be done differently are unmet when we leave the meeting room. There is no time for the destructive dynamics of cynicism when twenty-first-century markets are rapidly shifting business platforms from mass production to mass collaboration.

As shared understanding replaces control as the fundamental driver of business consistency, the conversations—and thus the meetings—have to be radically transformed such that listening is valued, ideas are depoliticized, differing views build on rather than clash with each other, and creative collective thinking displaces myopic groupthink. In short, for shared understanding and collaboration to become the primary drivers of business performance and for collective learning to become a core competency, meetings must become highly functional management tools.

In the mid-1990s, during my time with the Blue Cross Blue Shield Federal Employee Program (FEP), we recognized that, given the then new pace of change erupting across all industries, we needed to improve the effectiveness of our meetings and the quality of our corporate conversations if we were to remain the market leader in a faster business environment.

At the time, in 1998, the business alliance of thirty-nine independent Blue Cross and Blue Shield organizations provided private health insurance to more than 3.7 million federal employees and family members nationwide, with annual premium revenues of almost $7 billion. The unique management challenge we faced was bringing together these thirty-nine separate and sometimes competing organizations into a collaborative infrastructure to deliver a seamless uniform health insurance product. With so many independent moving parts in our operating model, meeting this challenge sometimes felt like "herding cats."

Previously, when the pace of change was slower, we had the time needed to work the usual politics of forming a consensus among so many autonomous partners. But with the emerging new pace of change and the well-publicized cost challenges in the healthcare industry, we knew we needed a more effective meeting mechanism to move us beyond the usual politics and to help us achieve faster and smarter consensus. Thus, we invented a meeting process we called the Work-Thru.

Work-Thru sessions are designed to address complex business issues by drawing upon an organization's best collective thinking and moving to a clear consensus on action in a very short period of time. Work-Thrus were born from the observation that some of the best meetings inside an organization are off-site sessions that are run by outside facilitators. However, so often the energy and follow-through are lost once everyone returns to the office and the facilitators move on. Well, we thought, what if we designed a meeting where the business leader takes on the role of facilitator? While this would present a challenging skills and role transition for the typical manager, what better way to shift the social structures and practices in support of building collaboration than to train managers to be skilled and competent facilitators?

We recognized that if we were going to work smarter and faster, we needed a meeting discipline that fostered better conversations, more effective listening, greater participation by all, better processing of ideas, real consensus, clear accountability, and focused action—all in a short period of time. The foundational concept behind the design of the Work-Thru was simple: The secret to extraordinary performance is better conversations inside organizations. (We'll discuss the Work-Thru in more depth in Chapter 6.)

Unfortunately, this simple secret is not practiced inside most companies. In many instances, meetings are nothing more than "hijack" experiences in which two or three people dominate the discussion in a battle of wills and a clash of ideas, and the remaining participants become mere spectators. In the absence of a true consensus, apparent agreements and compromises or—worse yet—dictated mandates are undercut as participants who have not been heard or who do not agree find acceptable bureaucratic ways to passively exert their influence.

The traditional meeting tends to be a competition of ideas, where the focus is on the sport of being right and where the ineffective acting out of passions divides the room into winners and losers—and the losers do not go complacently but rather find ways to thwart the hollow victories once everyone leaves the room. Even in those instances where the gatherings are not contentious, traditional meetings tend to yield less than the best decisions possible because the meeting structure is inadequate to process individual thinking into collective intelligence, and, thus, produces inadequate information.

Changing the way we work together in meetings is the most important change that businesses need to make if they are serious about learning how to manage at the pace of change. In the wiki world, conversation is the catalyst that drives the company. That's because better dialogue drives better knowledge, and the broad early involvement of many and diverse voices delivers faster and more reliable results. We are learning that in a hyper-connected world, the quality of conversations often determines the quality of work.

Resetting the Measures

If someone were to walk into your offices and ask the first ten people she met to identify your company's most important goal, would she hear the same goal ten times or ten entirely different goals? This is an important question because, if the conventional wisdom that we get what we measure is true, then the answers will likely distinguish those organizations that have clarity of purpose and are highly collaborative from those that are siloed, scattered, and unfocused.

Unfortunately, most hierarchical organizations are more likely to be siloed than collaborative. That's problematic because a company consisting of functional silos is not likely to have a highly integrated measurement system. Instead, its metrics are more likely to be an ad hoc collection of disconnected functional measures that, unfortunately, encourages people to work at cross-purposes. Consequently, the vast majority of workers cannot list their company's top goals and priorities. They know what their tasks and assignments are, but they cannot tell you how their work connects to the larger corporate effort. Without a shared understanding of the key priorities, ad hoc metrics tend to produce a cacophony of interpretations about what is important for the business.

An unfortunate consequence of the lack of clear measures of success is that many of today's knowledge workers are disengaged and underutilized. This is a confusing state of affairs for managers who feel that they have made a substantial effort to effectively communicate the company's top priorities through various communiqués and corporate forums. What these leaders fail to grasp is that knowledge workers understand and engage with goals only when they are involved in their creation. It is then that they're able to see how their contributions connect with the work of their colleagues, and they are also able to judge for themselves whether or not the goals make sense. Until knowledge workers are able to personally make this judgment, they do not engage with the goals no matter how many times these priorities are broadcast in one-way communications.

Unless organizations change their ways by using collective learning rather than central planning to set their goals and by building shared understanding rather than sending well-intentioned memos to solicit the workers' commitment to those objectives, they are likely to find themselves at a distinct competitive disadvantage in a new economy where only the innovative prosper. Without engagement, innovation is nearly impossible.

One of the prime contributors to the pervasive lack of clarity in traditional organizations is that they often have too many goals at one time. When new opportunities are continually arising in a fast-changing world and when organizations have not yet developed the collective learning processes to effectively narrow their focus on the right opportunities, managers often give in to the temptation to add one more critical initiative to an already overflowing plate. However, the problem with continually taking on more projects as the primary strategy for managing the new pace of change is that the greater the number of critical priorities, the less likely that any one of the initiatives will be accomplished with excellence.

FranklinCovey has quantified the relationship between the number of priority goals and the probability of excellent achievement. The company's research found that the likelihood of achieving all goals with excellence falls dramatically when there are more than three top priorities, and once the number of goals exceeds ten, there is no chance that any of the goals will be achieved with excellence.[2] In assessing these results, the late Stephen Covey concluded, "There's a key principle that many fail to understand about focusing an organization: People are naturally wired to focus on only one thing at a time (or at best very few) with excellence."[3]

The piling up of centrally planned initiatives is very problematic when organizations are trying to keep up with the challenges of managing in fast-changing times. Traditional organizations come from a long and successful history where managing complexity was about the effective control of a multitude of details. In the closed systems of the assembly lines, things worked well when each individual worker focused on and accomplished her specific tasks. However, in the wiki world, organizations are more likely to be open systems where fulfilling the business mission requires continual interaction and iteration with both workers and customers to create intelligence and to produce knowledge applications. In this context, managing complexity is less about the details and more about sorting through the multitudes of developments to determine which ones are inconsequential and which ones might reshape the market. In the wiki world, business is about working smarter, not harder. Consequently, a strategy that deals with change by dumping more priorities on the corporate plate, fragmenting the new work into another set of tasks, and focusing specific individuals on the new tasks is doomed to failure.

In today's dynamic business environment, organizations will not be able to manage at the pace of change unless they involve workers in the identification, selection, and evolution of the top priorities. By cultivating a common focus about what's most important, a company will provide its workers with the simple set of focused measures that they need to effectively self-organize their efforts and achieve consistent excellent results.

Measurement is the way that organizations define what is most important to the business. A good measurement system should clearly spotlight the critical few drivers of the company's success. That's because the primary purpose of measurement is to provide a common frame of reference to enable performance. Once a clear focus is defined, measurement systems can be effectively integrated so that each person can connect her individual efforts to a clear set of shared goals.

In setting these common objectives, it's absolutely essential that the leaders choose the right goals. This is an important area where managers need to embrace the wisdom of slowing down to move fast. Getting the goals right happens only when leaders are committed to a bias for results over a bias for action. They need to take the time to first understand and then measure, and avoid the bravado of setting premature goals based on impulse. While it may appear courageous and decisive, bravado is nothing more than bold action without understanding. And without understanding, managers are more likely to target what's easy rather than what's important to measure. For example, when digital downloading stifled the sales of compact discs, pushing album sales targets would have demonstrated a lack of understanding of the changing dynamics of the music industry. At the time, measuring the sales of CDs was easier than defining the new metrics of electronic file swapping. However, quantifying the activity of a new emerging business model was the more important measure.

The right goals are not derived from managerial impulse but rather reflect what's most important to customers. Thus, the leader's challenge is to facilitate effective learning processes that can sift through the complexities of evolving markets to correctly discover what is most important to their chosen customers. Once there is a shared understanding across the company around key customer values, then these attributes are translated into a simple set of meaningful measures to effectively guide the local behavior of the people who are closest to the consumers. Today's knowledge workers are capable of making local interdependent judgments once they have the right set of goals that they can use to bridge the analytical facts of the past with the changing circumstances of the present to create a consistent future.

THE PRACTICAL CHALLENGE

Managers today are truly living and working in unique and unfamiliar times. As the business landscape continues to be reshaped by the unprecedented combination of accelerating change, escalating complexity, and ubiquitous connectivity, managers find themselves caught between the tensions of two worlds—one that is stubbornly fading and the other that is rapidly emerging. Increasingly, they are feeling the pain of the reality that a nineteenth-century management model designed to reinforce the power and the influence of industry bosses no longer works in a world transformed by Twitter, Facebook, and YouTube. One disgruntled customer posting a pointed video on the Internet can render useless millions of dollars of brand advertising. Nevertheless, most managers—despite understanding that in a post-digital world, we really work for the customers and that power belongs to them—continue to report to traditional bosses who believe that power belongs to those in charge, and those bosses still write the paychecks. Until the bosses to whom they report can learn to let go of an old mindset and accept the uncomfortable reality that we are living in a new world with new rules, managers who understand the paradigm shift face a unique challenge in trying to bring real change to organizations that are not moving as fast as the world around them.

In a perfect world, everyone would adapt to the reality of change as it happens, and we would all have the wherewithal to let go of old ways when they no longer work. In a perfect world, we would change our beliefs when the evidence is clear that, regardless of how old assumptions may have been useful and worked in the past, new assumptions do a better job of explaining the world around us. But we don't live in a perfect world. Just as it took time in the sixteenth century for the majority of people to give up a thousand-year-old doctrine and accept Copernicus's observation that it was the earth that revolved around the sun and not the other way around, it will take time for business leaders to give up a hundred years of managerial belief by accepting the new reality that networks are smarter than hierarchies. But business leaders do not have that much time to make the transition because today's imperfect world moves far faster than it did in the sixteenth century.

For those managers who understand that despite their boss's preferences, a nineteenth-century management model is unsustainable in a twenty-first-century world, there are options available for them to effectively manage while navigating between two mindsets in an imperfect world. Later in the book, we will outline fifty different practices that managers can use to begin to transform their organizations. While some of these practices have been borrowed from newer companies that actively turned their backs on hierarchies and built their organizations as networks from the beginning, you will find that many of the practices have been developed in traditional organizations by managers who found a way to successfully navigate between the two mindsets.

Each of the subsequent five chapters describes in more depth the five disciplines and the 3 M's that are the foundation of the emerging Wiki Management model, as depicted in Figure 3-1. The chapters present practical examples that managers can consider using in their particular work settings. The practices provide examples of how to reset the managers, the

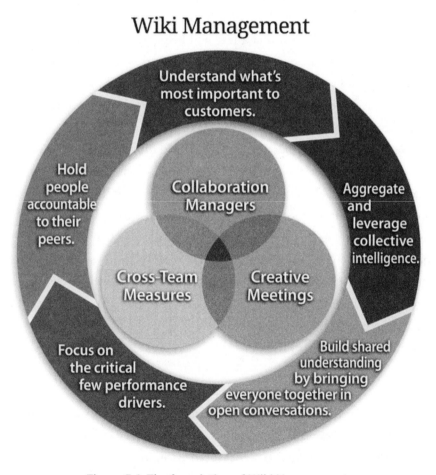

Figure 3-1. The foundation of Wiki Management.

meetings, and the measures to fully realize the value from each of the five disciplines.

In approaching these practices, you will probably find that some fit in your work environment and particular circumstances, while others may not. That's perfectly acceptable. The goal is not to implement all fifty practices but rather to identify those that could make a difference in your workplace. In each chapter, we encourage you to find the two or three practices that you could easily implement and to focus only on those. Your goal is to come up with a program built around the ten or so practices that you will be able to put in place. Ideally, the ten you select will be distributed across the 3 M's such that a few will help you to reset your role as a manager and become an effective facilitator, others will enable you to reset the meetings so you can tap into the power of your staff's collective intelligence, and still others will reinforce cross-functional collaboration as you reset the measures.

Getting on the right bus, letting go of an old mindset, and resetting the 3 M's means embracing an extraordinary level of change in the fundamental roles, relationships, and responsibilities of both managers and workers. It requires a radical transformation in how things get done in the workplace. As you become acquainted with the practices in the subsequent chapters, you will become familiar with methods and techniques that you can use to change the conversation, uncover your collective intelligence, and build the collaboration necessary to meet the challenges of a faster moving, hyper-connected world.

CHAPTER SUMMARY: KEY POINTS

→ Managing innovation is now a critical core competency across all industries. Whereas in the past innovations tended to be more incremental and happened at a measured pace, today innovation is more constant and clearly more disruptive.

→ The difference between being innovative and managing innovation is that, while any new entrant can be innovative by creating the next new thing, skillfully managing innovation is about moving from innovation to innovation.

→ Resetting the managers means accepting that the power to be connected is greater than the power to be in charge and transitioning the leader's role from being a boss to being a facilitator.

→ Resetting the meetings is about transforming business gatherings from ineffective political debating jousts to powerful channels of collective learning by including more people in open conversations.

→ Resetting the measures is accomplished by replacing disjointed metrics habits with a focused measurement discipline that collectively identifies the most important drivers of success and aligns key cross-functional goals with the delivery of customer value.

4

Understand What's Most Important to Customers

ave Carroll is a musician from Halifax, Nova Scotia. In the summer of 2008, Dave and his band were traveling on United Airlines to Omaha, Nebraska, where they were scheduled to perform. While they were sitting at the gate for their connecting flight at Chicago's O'Hare Airport, Dave heard someone behind him exclaim, "They're throwing guitars out there!" Dave's eyes widened in horror as he looked out the window just in time to see his $3,500 Taylor guitar sail through the air and crash to the ground. When he arrived at the baggage claim in Omaha, he confirmed his worse fears: The neck on his beloved six-string was split in two.

Fortunately for Dave and the band, none of their other instruments were damaged and they were able to fulfill their concert obligations. Once things settled down after the hectic activity of the setups, rehearsals, and performances, Dave placed a call to United to register his claim with the airline for the expensive repair of his guitar. He was stunned when the customer service representative told him that there was nothing that the airline could do to help him and that the repair was his responsibility. According to United's policy, all claims for damages must be filed within twenty-four hours, and Dave had missed the deadline. Dave protested that he had actually witnessed the irresponsible handling of his precious cargo and it was wrong for United to shirk its responsibility to its paying passengers by hiding behind a rigid policy. Despite his continued attempts over the next nine months, nobody up the chain of command would budge. The policy was quite clear, and policy compliance is what's most important to the bosses in large organizations.

In addition to being a talented musician, Dave also happens to be a fairly decent songwriter. Realizing that he was at the end of the line with United's brass, he literally took matters into his own hands by posting a YouTube video of him and his band playing an original song entitled "United Breaks Guitars." On its first day, the video received 150,000 hits. By day three, it had gone viral with more than 500,000 hits and caught the attention of United's executives. The airline had a change of heart and called Dave to let him know that it might be willing to make an exception to its policy. United also asked if Dave might consider taking down the video. Dave responded that there was no way he was removing what had suddenly become his best marketing tool. In addition to an increase in his musical bookings, Dave was receiving invitations to speak at corporate events on the importance of customer service. Dave's meteoric rise at the expense of what was once known as the "Friendly Skies" continues today with the original video approaching an astonishing thirteen million hits and the 2012 publication of his book on the power of one voice in the new world of social media.

If you're wondering if Dave ever received compensation for his damaged guitar, he did, but it came from an unexpected place. Bob Taylor, the owner of Taylor Guitars, was so pleased with all the free positive publicity his company was receiving from the video that he gave Dave two replacement guitars to express his gratitude.

The important lesson from this story is one that today's best businesses take very seriously. When one voice in a hyper-connected world can undo every dollar a company spends on brand imaging, you better appreciate that we no longer work for the bosses. In today's wiki world, we work for the customers. Perhaps no company understands this changing reality better than Zappos.

WORKING FOR THE CUSTOMER

Zaz Lamarr wanted to do something special for her mother, who was stricken with cancer. Zaz thought that a new pair of shoes might brighten her mother's spirits. However, given the weight loss that can happen with cancer patients, Zaz wasn't sure what size would fit her mom. So, she placed an online order with Zappos for several pairs of shoes in a variety of sizes, hoping at least one of them would work. Fortunately, two of the pairs fit, and Zaz made arrangements to return the remaining pairs of shoes to Zappos.[1] However, before Zaz was able to get to the UPS store, her mother took a sudden turn for the worse and passed away. When Zappos contacted Zaz after the shoes were not returned as expected, she explained that with all the arrangements she had to handle following her mother's death, she had been unable to comply with Zappos's return policy.

At Zappos, policies are guidelines, not rigid rules. When the customer service representatives became aware of Zaz's circumstances, rather than insisting that she needed to make time to go to the UPS store, they sent UPS to her.[2] While this gesture was very touching, what happened next is what caused this story to go viral on Facebook and Twitter, but for very different reasons than Dave Carroll's video went viral. Zappos customer service representatives got together and sent Zaz a beautiful bouquet of flowers to let her know that they were thinking of her in her time of need. At Zappos, policies are not restricted to protecting the company's interests. The popular online retailer also has policies for extending kindnesses to customers. That's because at Zappos, all employees know that they work for the customers and that their primary focus is to always understand what's most important to customers.

CUSTOMERS OVER BOSSES

Traditional large businesses, despite their rhetoric about how much they value their customers, have long histories of giving priority to what's most important to the bosses. Unfortunately, Dave Carroll's frustration is more common than the touching experience of Zaz Lamarr, especially in dealings with large organizations.

Innovative managers who practice the disciplines of Wiki Management know that the first responsibility of management is to understand what's most important to customers. The work of business no longer begins with planning around what the bosses think. In the wiki world, the starting point for business is always focused on what the customers value, and what's important to customers is oftentimes very different from what the company values.

Customer values are rarely found inside executive suites. In fast-changing times, only the most arrogant managers would forgo asking the question and presume they already know the answer to what's most important to customers. Customer values are discovered only outside the organization, and because they evolve and change, managers need to continually inquire and step outside their companies to be in step with fast-paced markets. Effective decision making requires organizations to have processes for actively listening to their customers and understanding what they value most. Michael Hammer makes the point, "When companies know only about themselves and not about their customers . . . they make all kinds of decisions with inadequate information."[3]

When you step outside your company, the first thing you have to do is to walk in your customers' shoes. You need to learn to see your organization and your products from their perspective. It is especially important for managers to get out of their offices and to go into the marketplace to meet their customers face-to-face. In the heyday of traditional management, many managers could go their entire careers without ever meeting an end user of their products. Their only contact with customers was usually through well-organized data in neatly prepared analytical reports.

While customer data is important, it is not enough. If you really want to know whom you're working for, you need to talk to customers, hear their voices, look them in the eye, and know how it feels for them to do business with you. Even if you spend only a couple of hours each month listening to service center calls, you need to take the time to directly connect with your customers' experience. As you listen to them, find out why they buy your products, and don't be surprised if they use them for different reasons than you had in mind. This kind of knowledge, which you can get only by engaging with your customers, is emotional intelligence, and you're not likely to find it in data charts and reports. Only when you walk in their shoes will you truly know the strength of your emotional bond with your customers and the power of your brand.

Zappos has built a powerful brand because all its workers know that emotional bonds are built by putting more importance on delighting customers than pleasing bosses. At Zappos, they don't just sell shoes; they also design their processes to make sure that everyone in the company takes the time to walk in the customers' shoes. Emotional bonds are human bonds. The touching humanity of sending flowers to Zaz Lamarr rather than insisting on policy is what caused the Zappos story to go viral. Perhaps the United Airlines story might have played out very differently if United workers were trained and encouraged to take a little time to walk in their customers' shoes before applying their policies.

SERENDIPITY OVER PLANNING

One of the core pillars of traditional management is planning. Planning provides comfort in the face of complexity because, by defining and sequencing a set of action steps, managers have a sense that a reliable path to a certain outcome has been put in place. Planning assumes that the world is stable and predictable.

For the most part, planning has proved to be a highly effective management tool because, until recently, the future was something managers could reasonably forecast. Planning can serve as the foundation of strategy when the future is clear or at least clear enough. In stable circumstances, planning and analysis generally do cultivate sound business decisions.

However, what happens when markets are not so stable and predictable and the pace of change continually accelerates? What happens when a steady stream of new technologies continually reshapes the business landscape? What happens when your business environment is no longer local or domestic and you find yourself competing in global and multicultural markets? What happens when the rules of the game change and you need to transform your organization from an Industrial Age establishment to a Digital Age innovator? In the exponential wiki world, where innovation, flexibility, and adaptability are necessities for business survival, linear planning methodologies that assume a known and stable business environment can no longer serve as the foundation for building strategies.

In a post-digital world, planning is no longer a strategic activity; it is now only a tactical exercise. Today's continually changing and uncertain markets make it impossible to predict the future much beyond the immediate horizon. Consequently, traditional long-term planning is likely to be counterproductive by locking businesses into what may become obsolete strategies or by blinding them from discerning the opportunities in newly emerging technologies or markets. If companies want to be ready for the future in fast-changing times, they need to learn how to leverage serendipity as a useful management tool.

Serendipity means finding things that we are not looking for that turn out to be very valuable. The word was first coined in the eighteenth century by the British writer Horace Walpole after he became familiar with the old Persian tale "The Travels and Adventures of Three Princes of Serendip." The tale relates the story of how the princes set out on a specific journey and accidently discover a whole series of clues that would later establish their innocence when they are falsely accused of a crime.[4] Serendipitous discoveries are not usually random events but rather connections or insights that occur when we are searching for one thing only to find something else. In moments of serendipity, we discover what we didn't know we didn't know.

When a company is focused on what's most important to the bosses, strategy is about enhancing the bosses' intelligence and then leveraging that intelligence through the construction of elaborate business plans. This was the practice at Microsoft during Bill Gates's tenure as CEO, when he would gather reports and analyses prepared by his staff and go off to a cabin in the woods, where he would spend a week by himself to craft the company's strategy. As long as the CEO and the company are changing as fast as the world around them—which was possible at the time of Gates's tenure—this approach to strategy can work. However, when the world is changing faster than the company, leveraging the intelligence of a single individual becomes a very risky proposition. In fast-changing times, the essence of strategic work is having the capacity to continually discover what we don't know that we don't know. Going off by oneself into the woods is not the most effective process for getting in touch with this important knowledge.

When a company is focused on what's most important to customers, the fundamental work of strategy is focused more on learning than planning. That's why Google doesn't engage in detailed long-term planning and its strategic horizon is about ninety days. Google understands that the world is changing fast and that a lot can happen to render fixed plans obsolete. By reassessing work in ninety-day increments, the managers and workers at Google are continually learning, providing opportunities to collectively discover what they don't know that they don't know, and using that knowledge to make adjustments to their evolving plans. Similarly, Agile software developers organize their work into short two- or three-week sprints that are designed to deliver a specific internal or external customer deliverable. At the end of each sprint, the developers and the business staff examine and evaluate the deliverable to make sure that the work is meeting customer expectations, discuss anything they may have learned since the last time they met, and make any needed adjustments to the deliverable for the next sprint. By working in smaller planning horizons, both Google and the Agile software developers are providing opportunities to leverage the power of serendipity to discover early on what they don't know that they don't know, and to use these learning moments to better adapt and respond to a fast-changing world.

PRACTICES

The following are actual practices used by companies to understand what's most important to customers. Given your role within your organization and the current state of your corporate culture, some practices may work better than others. Focus on the two or three practices that would best work in your particular business circumstances.

Resetting the Managers

PRACTICE #1: THINK OUTSIDE-IN. When innovative managers put the customer at the center of everything they do, they think differently than their traditional counterparts. Traditional managers often assume that everything that is needed to be successful out in the marketplace is contained inside the organization. As a consequence, these managers tend to think *inside-out* and view the outside world more as a conceptual market than as a collection of human customers.

Inside-out thinking reinforces the notion that bosses are more important than customers. This explains why traditional corporate cultures seem to be more interested in pleasing bosses than delighting customers. In the inside-out organization, the focus of business is on the *transaction*. As a result, we sometimes find that traditional managers don't attach any real value to their customers because consumers are viewed merely as market mechanisms for the transaction of products into profits.

Innovative managers, on the other hand, think *outside-in*. They understand that when they are working for the customers, they will never have everything they need to succeed within their walls. Outside-in organizations understand that managing at the new pace of change means that managers cannot rely solely on the knowledge of their inside experts. They assume that market reality is subject to accelerating change and that management's first job is to continually align its strategies and its products with what's most important to customers. In the outside-in organization, the focus of business is on the customer *experience*. Thus, if customer values are at odds with management policy, the first step of managers who think outside-in is usually to reconsider the value of the policy.

LEGO is a company that is thriving today because more than a decade ago, its people learned the value of thinking outside-in when they responded in an unusual way to a security breach. In the late 1990s, four weeks after the release of the first version of LEGO's Mindstorms kits, a student hacker cracked the software code for the new product and created a better version.[5] Rather than defensively protecting its copyright and beefing up its security, LEGO realized that the hacker meant no harm. In fact, the student was a loyal LEGO enthusiast who was only interested in making the product better. So, LEGO's managers decided to think differently by choosing to embrace rather than to fight the hacker and reaching out to all LEGO enthusiasts to invite them to cocreate the next generation of Mindstorms kits.

Today, LEGO supplements its 120 paid designers with 100,000 loyal enthusiasts.[6] Thinking outside-in has literally brought the company free resources. There's no better way to understand what's most important to customers than by inviting them to become voluntary cocreators, especially when they care about your products.

PRACTICE #2: MEET THE CUSTOMER. Every new hire at Zappos, whether it's the chief financial officer or a customer service representative, is required to begin employment by participating in the company's four-week customer training program. There are no exceptions.[7] While most companies state that listening to the voice of the customer is very important, Zappos actually backs up the commitment with an uncommon action—they actually answer the phone.

The call center is a special place at Zappos because it's where the employees get to meet the company's most important VIPs—their customers. There are no time limits on the calls, and the performance of customer service representatives is never measured by the number of calls per hour. What counts at Zappos is making sure that the telephone call is a positive experience for the customer, and if that takes several hours, that's all right as long as the customer's needs are being met.

Customers are not abstractions at Zappos. They are real people with real needs. That's why even the top executives are required to fully participate in the four-week customer service training. By understanding the value that Zappos places on creating a powerful customer experience and meeting customers on actual customer service calls, the executives learn firsthand what's most important to customers and come to appreciate that the fastest path to profits has more to do with creating value than cutting costs.

Any business that has a customer service area can implement this simple but powerful practice. Whether customer service is provided on the phone or through face-to-face interactions in retail outlets, there is ample opportunity for everyone in a company to have direct experience in understanding what matters most to the customers. When corporate cultures put a high value on making sure that everyone has an opportunity to meet the customers, that value pays rich dividends in designing affordable processes that continually delight customers. And delighted customers rarely move to the competition.

PRACTICE #3: ASK THE AUDIENCE. On the popular game show *Who Wants to Be a Millionaire*, one of the options available to contestants when they're having trouble coming up with the correct answer is to ask the audience members for their opinion. This onetime option is very valuable and safer than just making a guess on your own because the audience rarely gets the answer wrong. What if this option were available to retail businesses? Retail business owners have to make many guesses that have a direct effect on profitability. In the clothing business, for example, retail managers have to decide what items to stock and what quantities of each item to hold in their inventories. If they guess the fashion trends incorrectly and can't move particular items or if they underestimate the popularity of other items, their profits may be significantly diminished. Wouldn't it be nice if retailers could ask the audience for their opinion and stock only the exact number of items that will actually be sold?

In 2000, art students Jake Nickell and Jacob DeHart found a way to eliminate inventory risk when they invested $1,000 and started Threadless. Threadless is an online T-shirt company that found an innovative way to produce T-shirt designs that are guaranteed to sell. The founders' breakthrough idea was to sponsor weekly contests where customers are invited to submit T-shirt designs, which are then presented to the entire community of customers for a vote. Only the ten designs receiving the most votes are produced. To entice continued participation, fees are paid to the winning designers. Nickell and DeHart solved the inventory risk problem by forgoing top-down decision making and designing their company as a living network.

Threadless is an example of a company where understanding what's most important to the customer is the organizing principle of the business.

The leaders of this business are not bosses who rely on their individual expertise to make key decisions. Instead, Threadless's leaders are facilitators who have the capacity to leverage the collective intelligence of their customers, take the guesswork out of key decisions, and deliver exactly what the customer wants. Because Threadless has mastered the practice of asking the audience, it has become one of the world's most responsive companies.

PRACTICE #4: ONE AND DONE. When customers have a problem or need answers to important questions, there are few things that frustrate them more than the customer service gauntlet. We've all had the experience of calling a customer service number, only to be greeted by an automated system taking us through a series of prompts—none of which really describes our issue—before the recorded voice tells us to hold for an operator. Then, instead of a real person, we are greeted by another recorded voice informing us that there is an unusual volume of calls, apologizing for the delay, and telling us how important we are. After several minutes, we finally get to talk to a live human being who greets us with a pitch about the company's customer guarantee before asking us to describe our issue. Then, instead of reaching the resolution we are hoping for, the customer service representative explains that he does not have the authority to solve our issue, and he passes our call to another representative, who, in turn, passes us to another person until we eventually are passed back to the first representative, who empathizes with our plight and tells us he wishes there was something he could do. When we remind him of his opening pitch about the company's customer guarantee, we receive a firm lecture about how our particular problem is not covered by the guarantee. Despite a significant investment of our time, we end the call no happier than when we started.

At Zappos, customers never have to deal with the customer service gauntlet because the online retailer is committed to the practice of One and Done. The reason Zappos's customer service training lasts four weeks is to make sure that the company's frontline employees are the best informed individuals in the company and are fully trained to respond to any issue a customer may present. Zappos believes that customers should get their problems handled in one call by the person who answers the call. To back up this belief, every one of Zappos's customer service representatives has the authority to resolve customer issues without having to go through a supervisor or a manager.[8] At Zappos, the manager's job is not to be the sole authority on when to deviate from company policies, but rather to be a coach or a resource to guide the customer service representatives in exercising their own independent judgments in handling customer calls.

Zappos views calls into the customer service center as opportunities to create a customer experience rather than as costly transactions to be efficiently managed. That's why, in measuring the performance of the effectiveness of the call center—unlike most companies that focus on keeping the calls short by measuring what's known as the "average handle time"—the key metric at Zappos is the "average speed to answer." Zappos's goal is to answer 80 percent of calls within twenty seconds.[9]

One and Done is an opportunity to develop strong personal connections with customers and to provide the lasting memories that become the substance of a company's brand. Do you think that Zaz Lamarr will ever forget the random act of kindness she received from a fully empowered customer service representative the day Zaz told Zappos she couldn't return her recently deceased mother's shoes on time?

Resetting the Meetings

PRACTICE #5: JOIN THE CHAT. Some of the most important meetings about companies are happening outside their four walls. In these meetings, people that company personnel don't even know are making decisions that could catapult their enterprises to extraordinary success or sink them into oblivion. And what's most interesting is that many of these companies are not just absent from the meetings—they don't even know they're happening. We live in a new world with new rules, and one of the new rules of the wiki world is that social media has opened up a host of options for people to get together.

Neither United Airlines nor Taylor Guitars realized that Dave Carroll was convening millions of people on YouTube to highlight their services and products. While these social media proceedings were a serendipitous blessing for Taylor Guitars, United Airlines was blindsided by the unwelcome attention of this large impromptu business gathering.

When we worked for the bosses, the most important gatherings happened in staff and board meetings inside companies. However, now that we work for the customers, we know that managers cannot afford to absent themselves from the virtual meetings where customers are either building or harming the company brand. If we want to participate in these meetings, we need to Join the Chat.

While managers increasingly recognize the importance of becoming a part of the social network, becoming an effective voice in cyberspace requires much more than setting up a Twitter or LinkedIn account or building a Facebook page. If businesses want to have their voices heard in the virtual world, they have to abandon their traditional practices of trying to control conversations through broadcast and spin, and they must humbly embrace the dynamics of listen and learn. In meetings on the social network, the company voices that are heard belong to those that listen first. Traditional broadcast communications do not work well in social media.

The most successful managers on the social network are those who listen, observe, and are accepting of the thoughts and perspectives of their customers. This means that in implementing this practice, you need to assume a nondefensive stance. Joining the chat works best when you are more focused on understanding your customers than in making sure that the customers understand your company's position or policies. To effectively Join the Chat, in addition to setting up your own social media accounts, you also need to join and participate in the accounts others have created to talk about your company because it is in those spaces that you are most likely to build trust with your customers.

Zappos reinforces its bond with its customers by assigning staff members to be available to respond to Twitter activity twenty-four hours a day.[10] Countless numbers of people witness these staff members genuinely and nondefensively handle hundreds of customers' questions every day. In the social network, your "walk" counts much more than your "talk," which may explain why Zappos doesn't do broadcast advertising but invests heavily in all forms of customer service, including joining the chat.

PRACTICE #6: INNOVATION JAMS. Another way to discover what's most important to your customers is to engage them in a meeting with your staff to provide input for the development of your business. This is what IBM does using a practice the company invented known as Innovation Jams. IBM is using the Internet to bring fresh ideas into its walls by inviting more than 100,000 customers, outside consultants, and employee family members to join in shaping the future direction of the business. Periodically, Big Blue hosts these online forums where the participants are encouraged to offer their ideas and brainstorm on important business issues that affect the lives of its customers. IBM populates the Innovation Jam website with an array of background information on various industry topics to seed the online gathering. Innovation Jams have given IBM access to valuable collective intelligence by providing a vehicle for the company to aggregate the diverse, independent, and localized reflections of key customers. By employing this learning process as a foundation for navigating the business, IBM managers have real-time access to a range of ideas and knowledge far beyond the limits of the company's organizational walls, as well as a valuable pathway to staying in touch with what matters most to their customers.

PRACTICE #7: CUSTOMER PROXIES. Customer Proxies is a practice we used when we were designing new products or developing new systems in the Blue Cross Blue Shield Federal Employee Program. At the start of these special projects, we would bring together a cross section of people from various disciplines for an all-day facilitated session to build a solid shared understanding around the work to be performed.

In designing these sessions, we always invited people from our sales and customer service areas to participate as customer proxies because it wasn't practical or possible for us to invite actual customers into our sessions. This practice was especially important when we designed systems because there is often a natural tendency for software engineers to construct applications around capabilities that may be more meaningful to them than they are to the customers. Inviting customer proxies to our sessions was how we made sure we never lost sight of the fact that everything we did ultimately touched a customer.

PRACTICE #8: CLARIFYING QUESTIONS. Clarifying Questions is a practice that can be easily used in almost any meeting session. Clarifying questions are those that help meeting participants clearly understand a speaker's point of view and help make sure that everyone in the room has correctly heard what the speaker intended. This practice is especially useful in an initial discussion of controversial, emotional, or innovative ideas because it prevents the discussion from being hijacked by advocates of opposing viewpoints, who may become locked in a polarized debate.

Hijacked meetings easily disintegrate into a competition of ideas where the focus is on being right and where the ineffective acting out of passions divides the room into winners and losers. The losers do not just retreat quietly. Instead, once the meeting is over, they find ways to thwart whatever hollow victories were won. When the world is changing faster than your organization, the last thing you need as a manager is to find yourself in a hijacked meeting. Clarifying Questions is a simple practice that can effectively thwart the hijack.

In opening the meeting, the leader advises the group that each speaker presenting an idea will do so without interruption and that the opening presentation is neither the time nor the place for the expression of the participants' opinions, observations, and concerns—that will come later in the meeting. For the moment, the focus is on making sure that all participants understand the presenter's thoughts and ideas, not whether they agree, disagree, or have a different point of view.

After the speaker completes the presentation, the leader invites the group to ask clarifying questions and reminds the group once again that the time for agreements, disagreements, and other opinions will come later in the meeting. The purpose of the clarifying questions is solely to make sure that everyone has heard what the speaker intended.

Beginning meetings with uninterrupted presentations and clarifying questions radically changes the group dynamics of the gathering because it structures listening into the start of the meeting. The simple reason so many corporate meetings get hijacked is because most people don't begin meetings by listening to each other. They are usually focused on looking for openings to express their own opinions or to work their agenda or— worse yet—they are mentally absent as two or three individuals dominate the meeting and won't let anyone else speak. Having a period of clarifying questions after speakers have introduced their ideas means the participants have no choice but to listen and to understand what was presented. It puts in place the simple provision that before we agree or disagree or express another opinion, let's be sure that we've heard what's being said first.

When organizations embrace habits that emphasize the importance of listening, understanding, and collaboration, they create climates where colleagues view each other as mutual customers rather than as competitive advocates. If managers want to build a customer-focused company, facilitating an environment of mutual customers is a good place to start because the way workers respond to the company's customers is often a reflection of the way they treat each other.

Resetting the Measures

PRACTICE #9: BALANCED SCORECARDS. One of the most important contributions to the practice of business measurement is the recent development of the Balanced Scorecard by Robert Kaplan and David Norton.[11] The Balanced Scorecard is a one-page integrated picture of a business, project, or initiative that enables all involved to align their individual activities with a common set of simple measures. The scorecard contains twelve to twenty carefully selected measures that track organizational performance across four balanced perspectives: financial, customer, internal business processes, and learning and growth.[12] These selected key indicators provide a meaningful template for interpreting and understanding the interrelationships among the key components of business success.

A powerful attribute of the Balanced Scorecard is its inclusion of both outcome and driver measures. Outcome measures are lagging indicators that describe final results. Driver measures, on the other hand, are leading indicators that quantify the levels of performance of the key activities that strongly influence the ultimate outcomes. An effective Balanced Scorecard is a mixture of related lagging and leading indicators that reflect the fundamental strategy of the business, project, or initiative. When properly constructed, the driver measures provide reliable and actionable information about how and if the expected outcomes are being achieved, while the outcome measures provide the data necessary to continually validate whether or not the observed relationships between driver and outcome measures continue to hold true.

In the absence of such a tool, many traditional managers rely on their financial statements as their basic management measurement tool. This can be a dangerous practice because, for the most part, financial statements are collections of outcome measures that are not actionable. Financial statements are like final scores in a sporting event: Once the contest is over, there's nothing that any of the players can do to change the outcome. Financial statements are poor management tools because by the time you get the measures, there's nothing managers can do to impact the numbers. And more important, financial statements rarely reflect what's most important to customers.

The Balanced Scorecard is a powerful management tool because the focal point of the tool is the set of customer measures. The implicit logic in the scorecard recognizes that successful companies begin by understanding what's most important to their customers, then they build operations to deliver what their customers value most and set up learning processes to keep pace with market developments so they can continually grow the business. Positive financial results are the reward that companies receive when they are learning as fast as the world is changing and maintaining business processes that continually meet or exceed customer expectations. If there's a problem with the financial results, there's likely a problem in how the company is meeting what's most important to customers. (You can learn more about the Balanced Scorecard from Kaplan and Norton's book of the same name.)

PRACTICE #10: NET PROMOTER SCORE. Walk into any Apple Store and you immediately know that you have entered a special place. Apple Stores aren't just retail outlets; they are community centers where aficionados of Apple products gather to see what's new, learn more about their cherished gadgets, visit a Genius Bar to get a question answered, or just take in the experience of being around other Apple lovers. When Apple opened its first retail stores in 2001, market analysts feared that the company's foray into the retail space would be a drain on its profitability. Based on the standard retail industry metric of sales per square foot and the historical data of similar companies, the financial analysts were near unanimous in predicting the failure of the Apple Stores. The analysts couldn't have been more wrong. Today, with more than 395 stores worldwide, Apple has become one of the world's leading retailers.

How is it that Apple succeeded in an unfamiliar place and so many of the experts were wrong? The reason is a motto the technology company takes very seriously: *Think different*. The analysts predicted failure because they viewed business through the lens of the transaction and didn't appreciate the important distinction between good profits and bad profits. To the analysts, all profits were the same, and existing profitability data didn't support this strategic move. The managers at Apple, on the other hand, viewed their business through the lens of the experience, and they understood that when companies create a great experience that delights customers beyond their wildest expectations, the customers keep coming back and they bring their friends with them. What the analysts couldn't see—because it wasn't an item on the balance sheet—is that, by focusing on the experience over the transaction, Apple was able to leverage its customers into a free army of sales representatives to realize an extraordinary level of good profits. Apple understands that the key to being profitable has more to do with delivering customer value than it does with making money.

Fred Reichheld is a consultant at Bain & Company who noticed that companies that focus on good profits behave differently and are more successful than those that tolerate making bad profits. Reichheld defines good profits as net revenues realized by so delighting customers that they are willing to come back for more and bring their friends and colleagues with them.[13] Bad profits, according to Reichheld, are dollars made at the expense—and sometimes even at the abuse—of the customer.[14] Not surprisingly, Reichheld's research shows that companies that are more interested in earning good profits rather than just making money enjoy both strong profits and sustainable growth.[15]

Understanding the wisdom of "you get what you measure," Reichheld developed a simple but powerful measure that ensures that managers are primarily focused on delivering customer value and making good profits. The Net Promoter Score is a primary driver of success in many innovative companies including Apple, Zappos, LEGO, American Express, Intuit, GE, eBay, Facebook, Southwest Airlines, and JetBlue Airways.[16] All of these companies use the Net Promoter Score as a guide to making sure they always understand what's most important to customers.

The Net Promoter Score is based on the aggregation of the responses to a single question, using a scale of 0 to 10: "How likely is it that you will recommend this company or product or service to a friend or colleague?" Those who respond with a 9 or 10 are classified as Promoters. These are loyal customers who will make repeat purchases and enthusiastically make referrals to everyone they know. People who rate the company a 7 or 8 are designated as Passives. While basically satisfied, they are less likely to make unsolicited referrals. Detractors are customers who give a rating of 6 or below and are either dissatisfied or even angry with the company. The score is computed by calculating the percentage of customers who are Promoters and then subtracting the percentage that are Detractors. The highest possible score is a 100, which would occur if every customer rated the company a 9 or 10. On the other hand, if every customer were to rate the business a 6 or below, the score would be a negative 100.

According to Scott Cook, the founder of Intuit, there are two requirements for growth: happy customers and profitable customers. The Net Promoter Score helps Intuit keep its customers happy by always staying in touch with what matters most to the users of the company's products. In addition, it helps the company to sustain profitability year after year by making sure that its money is made from good profits.

PRACTICE #11: RESULTS-BASED/VALUES-BASED GOALS. In most companies, the fundamental unit of work is the performance of individual tasks. This task orientation is reinforced by traditional organization charts and their functional departments. In task-oriented companies, workers work for the boss, focus on tasks, and contribute to the completion of activities. Accordingly, traditional performance metrics have emphasized the measurement of tasks and activities.

However, from a customer's perspective, the performance of individual tasks does not necessarily result in delivering value. All of us can think of an example when we as customers encountered an individual in a company who wanted us to appreciate that he did his job right—that is, completed his tasks correctly—even though others' failures to complete their tasks meant that we did not get the result we expected. When it comes to delivering customer value, the fundamental unit needs to be the business process because customers receive value only when the entire process works. Companies that understand that business is about creating experiences rather than managing transactions focus on processes, not tasks. That's why their individual performance metrics are built around results-based and values-based goals rather than activity-based metrics.

Activity-based metrics measure the timely completion of discrete tasks that are usually within the relative control of the workers. An example is the requirement to handle a customer service call within a set number of minutes. The problem with activity-based goals is they don't necessarily correlate with good performance because it's possible to receive positive scores (quick calls) regardless of how satisfied or dissatisfied the caller may be with the interaction.

Results-based or value-based measures, on the other hand, are geared to make sure that customers receive the value they are expecting by the end of the call. Using a metric such as the Net Promoter Score is a better indicator of the effectiveness of a call center because it measures customers' satisfaction or dissatisfaction.

CHAPTER SUMMARY: KEY POINTS

→ The starting point for business is always focused on what the customers value, and what's important to customers is oftentimes very different from what the bosses value.

→ In a post-digital world, planning is no longer a strategic activity; it is now only a tactical exercise. Today's continually changing and uncertain markets make it impossible to predict the future much beyond the immediate horizon.

→ In fast-changing times, the essence of strategic work is having the capacity to continually discover what we don't know that we don't know.

→ When a company is focused on what's most important to customers, the fundamental work of strategy is focused more on learning than planning.

→ Positive financial results are the reward companies receive when they are learning as fast as the world is changing and maintaining business processes that continually meet or exceed customer expectations. If there's a problem with the financial results, there's likely a problem in how the company is meeting what's most important to customers.

5

Aggregate and Leverage
Collective Intelligence

On January 2, 2001, Larry Sanger met his old friend Ben Kovitz for dinner at a small Mexican restaurant in San Diego. It would be the dinner that would change the world. It had been almost a year since Sanger had come to Southern California to work as the editor in chief for Nupedia, a start-up online encyclopedia. Nupedia's founder, Jimmy Wales, had come up with the novel idea of using the platform of the budding Internet to solicit volunteers who would contribute articles to build a free encyclopedia. However, by the end of 2000, the seven-step peer review process that Sanger and his academic advisers had designed had produced only a handful of articles. At this glacial rate, Wales and Sanger were both concerned about the viability of their ambitious project.

As Kovitz empathized with Nupedia's predicament, he urged Sanger to take a look at the WikiWikiWeb site, an innovative but obscure computer program developed by software engineer Ward Cunningham to provide individual programmers with the ability to pool their knowledge and create common staples for the software community.[1] The break-through concept behind Cunningham's innovation was the then radical practice of allowing any coder to edit any page on the site. WikiWikiWeb was open to all who wanted to contribute, and to encourage participation, the coders were not required to have either an account or a password. The "wiki," as it came to be known among its early aficionados, was designed to be a transparent dialogue where software engineers could leverage their collective knowledge. To help facilitate a cohesive conversation, each wiki page had the ability to record and retain every edit so that anyone access-ing the site could see the iterative development of the software concepts. This unusual proclivity for transparency caught the attention of computer technicians, who quickly flocked to the new site.

Given its ease and transparency, Kovitz suggested that the wiki page just might be the solution for how large numbers of volunteers could quickly produce and edit a high volume of encyclopedia articles. For Sanger, this was one of those "lightbulb" moments. Kovitz's suggestion was a complete paradigm shift in the way encyclopedias could be built. Up until this point, Sanger's management model for building Nupedia was based on conventional protocols, where articles go through a sequential series of reviews by a hierarchy of experts. In that "lightbulb" moment, it became very clear to Sanger that the fundamental obstacle to Nupedia's sustainability was its seven-step hierarchical review process. He realized that if the online encyclopedia was to succeed, it had to become an open network with the capability for real-time editing steered by the collective wisdom of the masses rather than the conventional wisdom of the experts.

Sanger enthusiastically shared his insights with Wales, who quickly recognized how an open system approach might solve the online encyclo-pedia's problems. Thus, on January 10, 2001, Wales added wiki software to the Nupedia website.[2] However, not everyone in the Nupedia organiza-tion was as enthusiastic as Sanger and Wales. The academic experts were vigorously opposed to the notion that the masses could provide any value to a scholarly pursuit. The academics were professionals, and they were adamant that a collaboration with the crowd could never meet their high quality standards. Consequently, just five days later, on January 15, 2001, Wales removed the wiki software from Nupedia and launched a second independent project, which Sanger dubbed Wikipedia.[3]

We all know what happened from there. The meteoric growth of Wikipedia is well documented, and most of us have never heard of Nupedia. While the experts continue to debate the quality of the online encyclopedia, all of us are amazed that the world's largest and most widely used reference work continues to be built by a self-organized collaboration of the masses. Perhaps none are more amazed than those most affected by the dinner that changed the world—the editors at the *Encyclopedia Britannica*, who announced on March 13, 2012, that after 244 years, the reference book was going out of print.

Another traditional institution that recently discovered the astounding power of collective intelligence is the scientific research community. In the summer of 2011, Firas Khatib, a biochemist at the University of Washington, felt something needed to be done to accelerate the progress of solving a molecular puzzle that had stumped the world's best scientists for more than a decade. The evasive puzzle involved figuring out the detailed molecular structure of a protein-cutting enzyme from an AIDS-like virus found in monkeys. Because this enzyme plays an important role in the spread of the virus, Khatib knew that figuring out its structure could be the breakthrough needed to arrest the medical malady. That's when Khatib turned to Foldit.

Foldit is a collaborative online video game developed by the University of Washington that enlists players worldwide to solve difficult protein-structure problems.[4] There are no special requirements for joining the Foldit community. All comers are welcome, which explains why most of the more than 235,000 Foldit players have little or no background in biochemistry.[5] Khatib recognized that the molecular challenge was a good fit for the capabilities of the Foldit game. Incredibly, what had evaded the world's best individual scientific experts for ten years was solved by the collective knowledge of a diverse group of online gamers within only ten days. When you have the capability to aggregate and leverage collective intelligence, you discover that there are many times when diversity trumps ability.

THE WISDOM OF CROWDS

James Surowiecki, in his insightful book *The Wisdom of Crowds*, provides numerous examples of where, under the right conditions, groups are highly intelligent and consistently outperform even the smartest individuals in them.[6] In his study of collective intelligence, Surowiecki found that if four conditions are satisfied, groups can provide incredibly sound and accurate judgments.[7]

The first condition is diversity of opinion. Having different perspectives—even eccentric notions—broadens the available information, provides the capacity for evolving ideas, makes it easier for individuals to be candid, and protects against the negative dynamics of shortsighted groupthink.

The second condition is independent thinking, which means that each individual is free to express her own opinions without editing and without any pressure to conform to the beliefs of others in the group. Surowiecki makes the point that "paradoxically, the best way for a group to be smart is for each person in it to think and act as independently as possible."[8]

The third condition is local knowledge. In order to truly access collective knowledge, the group must be able to draw upon specialized and localized intelligence because the closer a person is to the problem or the customer, the more likely she is to have a meaningful contribution. This is why social networks such as the Internet, which include large numbers of people and where no one is in charge, are so valuable. They allow important information to quickly and freely flow from the fringe to the core.

The fourth and final condition is aggregation mechanisms. Without the capacity to collate and integrate the diverse and independent thinking of large numbers of people, there is only chaos and cacophony. Surowiecki emphasizes that "a decentralized system can only produce genuinely intelligent results if there's a means of aggregating the information of everyone in the system."[9] Aggregation mechanisms are processes or systems for learning the integrated content of collective knowledge. By quickly collecting the decentralized observations of its many stakeholders and discerning the inherent patterns and trends, organizations are able to use the collective intelligence of the masses to solve difficult problems or to guide highly effective execution, as the biochemists and the editors of Wikipedia have convincingly shown us.

NOBODY IS SMARTER THAN EVERYBODY

Technological advances, especially since the arrival of the Internet, are expanding the possibilities for systems architects to create platforms for aggregating and leveraging collective intelligence. For example, Amazon uses its online data to construct its own bestseller lists and to publish consolidated ratings of books by its customers. eBay keeps vendors in its online market honest by collecting, collating, and publishing buyers' ratings of the sellers. This real-time access to the available collective wisdom of all the buyers makes purchasing on the Web a better customer experience.

No single expert or even group of experts can come anywhere close to matching the completeness of knowledge or the incredible speed of a well-designed electronic learning platform that can aggregate the wisdom of the crowd. Before the Internet, we were substantially limited in our ability to quickly access the collective intelligence of the larger community. Although it has always been true that nobody is smarter than everybody, because we had lacked the technology to organize the intelligence of large numbers of people, access to collective knowledge was simply not practical. Thus, in the days before the Web, seeking out the expertise of the brightest among us was the most expeditious course for navigating business success. However, the current state-of-the-art technology is making it perilous for organizations to endeavor to meet today's market challenges by relying on the judgments of a handful of experts.

The systems architectures at Amazon, eBay, and Google are examples of how the Internet is dramatically revolutionizing the business landscape. In addition to Web-enabled technologies that transform simple transaction information into collective intelligence, the Internet has opened up a whole new world of possibilities for creating electronic learning platforms that allow organizations to reach out to incredibly large numbers of people and to effectively engage all willing participants in collaborative dialogue. Why limit your strategic learning to the knowledge of a handful of executives within your organizational walls when some of the most intelligent people in the world are eager and willing to work with you—sometimes even for free! When the market demands increased knowledge and speed, the more voices you can get into the same room at the same time, the better the knowledge and the faster you can transform that knowledge into execution—provided that you have workable collective learning processes. Web-based learning platforms are furnishing an unprecedented capacity for organizations to reach outside their walls and expand the available knowledge in their strategic conversations.

THE GOLDCORP CHALLENGE

Another company that discovered the power of using the Internet to reach beyond its walls and expand the strategic conversation is the Canadian gold producer Goldcorp Inc. In the late 1990s, Rob McEwen, then Goldcorp's CEO, was wondering if he had made a big mistake five years earlier when he acquired a fifty-year-old gold mine in Red Lake, Ontario, that yielded lots of rocks but not many nuggets. In fact, facing increasing production costs, mounting debts, and almost no productivity, Goldcorp had been forced to cease mining operations at the mine.[10] Although it seemed as if the best days of the Red Lake mine were long behind, McEwen was convinced that there had to be substantial undiscovered deposits of ore somewhere beneath the 55,000-acre site. All Goldcorp had to do was find them. And so, McEwen invested $10 million in exploration and sent his geologists prospecting on a last-ditch expedition.

Although the geologists were skeptical, they nevertheless gave the exploration their best efforts and were pleasantly surprised a few weeks later to bring back some astounding news: Test drilling in nine of the exploratory holes suggested vast deposits of new gold with an average concentration of ore as much as thirty times richer than Goldcorp was currently producing.[11] However, this remarkable discovery did not solve the productivity problem. While the geologists had found strong indications of fresh gold, there was still the question of finding the exact location of the ore, and that would require deep drilling, which is much more costly than test drilling.

After a year of further exploration, running up more costs, and not locating the elusive ore, a frustrated McEwen decided he needed to step away and take a break from the office. He enrolled in a weeklong program about trends in information technology that MIT was sponsoring for presidents and CEOs. Part of the program was an orientation on Linux and open source software. McEwen was fascinated by the story of how Linus Torvalds had used the Internet to build a world-class computer operating system written by volunteer programmers located all over the globe. By the end of the lecture, McEwen was convinced that he had found the solution to the problem of locating the elusive gold at Red Lake. If Goldcorp's geologists couldn't locate Red Lake's new gold, perhaps the company could open the exploration process and invite drilling strategies from geologists around the globe.

As soon as McEwen arrived back at his Toronto office, he outlined his plan to Goldcorp's geologists and executives. The company would sponsor a contest with a total of $575,000 in prize money to be divided among three finalists and twenty-five semifinalists submitting the best drilling plans to help the company achieve its goal of locating six million ounces of gold. Goldcorp would take the unprecedented step of posting every bit of information about its 55,000-acre site on its website. This included fifty years' worth of maps, charts, and reports, as well as detailed geological data. Goldcorp would use the power of the Internet as a learning platform to reach out to the worldwide community of geologists and engineers to locate the elusive gold.

The immediate reaction of Goldcorp's geologists and executives to McEwen's plan was shock. They were aghast to think that the company would make public all its proprietary data, and they were concerned about how Goldcorp's geologists would be viewed by members of the scientific community when they learned that the company was sponsoring a contest to prospect its gold. The Goldcorp staff shared the traditional mindset of Industrial Age corporations that believe the smartest company is the one with the smartest individuals, and it keeps its knowledge to itself as a competitive advantage. They felt that the contest would fly in the face of conventional wisdom and would publicly embarrass Goldcorp's geologists before their professional peers. Goldcorp's staff, it seemed, was more concerned about looking smart than being smart.

McEwen was not to be rebuffed. In the wake of his MIT experience, he understood that conventional wisdom is no substitute for collective wisdom. Goldcorp needed to abandon its nineteenth-century thinking and catapult into twenty-first-century technology if it was to have any hope of turning itself around. Thus, the "Goldcorp Challenge" was launched in March 2000. The enthusiastic response from the international community of scientists and geologists was immediate. The Challenge website received more than 475,000 hits, and more than 1,400 online prospectors from fifty-one countries registered as Challenge participants. Within weeks, submissions from all over the world were appearing on Goldcorp's virtual doorstep, and by the contest deadline, the company had received detailed drilling plans from more than 140 participants.

The Challenge identified 110 geological targets, more than half of which had not been previously nominated by Goldcorp's geologists. More than 80 percent of the designated targets were found to be rich in new gold with a yield of more than eight million ounces, far exceeding Goldcorp's initial goal of six million ounces. Astoundingly, at the March 2001 Goldcorp Challenge awards presentation, McEwen was able to proudly announce that Goldcorp was once again profitable and debt-free!

When McEwen first came up with the idea for the Goldcorp Challenge, all he was hoping for was a way to locate the new gold at the Red Lake site. What he did not anticipate was the astonishing and unexpected learnings from the contributions of the Challenge participants that would revamp the company's mining business model. In presenting the awards to the contest winners, McEwen acknowledged, "These individuals and teams represent the leading edge of mining in the twenty-first century. We congratulate them on their initiatives, skills, and understanding of how new economy tools are transforming the mining industry."[12]

The Goldcorp Challenge taught McEwen an important lesson about knowledge as an economic asset: Knowledge is an abundant, not a scarce, resource. Before the contest, Goldcorp was mired in an Industrial Age mindset that believes organizations need to compete for scarce resources and should hold their most important knowledge as proprietary to maintain their competitive advantage. McEwen learned that because knowledge is an abundant resource, the only way that it grows is by giving it away. He was amazed at the number of innovative ideas that Goldcorp received by making its once proprietary data available on the Internet. By sharing its trade secrets with the world's scientific community, Goldcorp was able to tap into a rich diversity of technical expertise beyond the borders of its organization, and in the process, it significantly expanded the wealth of its corporate knowledge in addition to paring two to three years from its expected exploration time. "We have done something nobody has ever done before in the mining industry and in the process fundamentally changed the way Goldcorp thinks about mining," says McEwen. "We have created a new exploration frontier for Red Lake and have given the international mining community a model to work with that we have proven to be successful."[13]

NETWORKS OVER HIERARCHIES

For more than a century, human organizations have been built upon the assumption that the smartest organization is the one with the smartest individuals, and for all that time, this notion worked remarkably well. This explains why, when it comes to organizing the work of large numbers of people, we have invariably built command-and-control structures. The fundamental premise of hierarchies is that by giving the smartest individuals the power to command and control the work of others, we make average employees work far more effectively than they would if left to their own judgments.

However, Wikipedia, Amazon, eBay, Google, and Goldcorp are challenging the continued wisdom of this longstanding assumption. Wikipedia and Goldcorp, which at first blindly followed traditional hierarchical thinking, learned painfully the limitations of chasing supposed experts. It was only when they radically shifted gears that they each stumbled into a new way of thinking far better suited for a world suddenly reshaped by accelerating change. Amazon, eBay, and Google—all of which were formed after the advent of the Digital Revolution—deliberately eschewed hierarchical structures in building their new companies. All of them discovered that the key to extraordinary performance was learning how to harness the wisdom of crowds. Today's best-run companies fully appreciate that in a hyper-connected world, the smartest organizations are those that know how to aggregate and leverage collective intelligence.

As we continue to transition into the Digital Age, it will become obvious to more companies that no single individual or even an elite cadre of star performers can adequately process the ever-evolving knowledge of fast-changing markets into operational excellence in real time. Star performers are inadequately equipped for the task of organizing large numbers of people in fast-changing, complex markets. When technological advances make networks smarter and faster than hierarchies, self-organizing teams of workers with diversified skills consistently out-perform those whose work is organized and directed by persons in authority.

The increasing superiority of networks should not be misconstrued as repudiation of individual intelligence. Quite the contrary. Individual intelligence is vital to the aggregation of collective intelligence. The conditions of diversity of opinion, independent thinking, and local knowledge that Surowiecki defines as critical ingredients in collating collective intelligence are all dimensions of individual intelligence. What distinguishes networked organizations from their hierarchical counterparts is that, while hierarchies leverage the individual intelligence of a selected few, networks leverage the collective intelligence of the many smart people spread throughout their organizations.

PRACTICES

The following are actual practices used by companies to aggregate and leverage the collective intelligence within their organizations. Given your role within your organization and the current state of your corporate culture, some practices may work better than others. Focus on the two or three practices that would best work in your particular business circumstances.

Resetting the Managers

PRACTICE #12: CHOOSE YOUR COLLEAGUES. The basic concept behind this practice is that employees should have a voice in the selection of their coworkers. Historically, the hiring decision has been the prerogative of the supervisor, typically without any input from the people who will be working with the new hire. When a potential candidate does meet with someone other than the hiring supervisor, it's usually with an internal recruiter from the human resources department or the hiring supervisor's boss.

Whole Foods hires differently. Its leaders understand that getting the right people on their teams is one of the most important drivers of business performance. That's why when you apply for a position at Whole Foods, whether or not you get the job depends upon the vote of the team you'll be working with.

The hiring process at Whole Foods is designed to leverage the collective intelligence of the full team rather than relying on the individual judgment of a single supervisor. Thus, candidate interviews generally include both the team leader and a panel of peers. CEO John Mackey feels that the team interview process is the most effective way to make hiring decisions because the diversity of the panel of peers is a better way to assess the match of the prospective job candidate with the different aspects of the roles and responsibilities of the position. According to Mackey, "Anyone is capable of fooling a team leader for a while, but it is much more difficult to deceive the entire team."[14]

Once a candidate is selected to begin work at Whole Foods, the hiring process is not over; in fact, it's really just begun. New hires start with a thirty- to ninety-day orientation period in which they attend training classes and learn all the aspects of their particular jobs. During this time, the team members get a more complete picture of how the recruits will contribute to the success of the team. This is important because every four weeks, the productivity of teams in every Whole Foods store is measured, and those teams whose numbers exceed performance thresholds are awarded bonuses in their next paycheck. Teams cannot afford to have any slackers if they want to contend for these performance bonuses.

The hiring process concludes with a final team vote at the end of the orientation period. A recruit wins a full-time spot on the team by receiving a two-thirds majority vote of the teammates. The team leader has the same vote as everyone else on the team, which means that without the two-thirds majority, the new hire is let go even if the team leader voted to keep her.

Whole Foods believes that the best hiring decisions happen when those who will be most directly affected are the ones making the decision. That's why the company has reset the role of the manager in the recruiting of team members, and it may explain why Whole Foods is perennially voted by its team members as one of *Fortune* magazine's 100 "Best Companies to Work For."

PRACTICE #13: LEAD BY FACILITATION. The essence of this practice is a substantial shift in the stance of how executive leaders hold power. The best leaders today are increasingly facilitators, not bosses. Like Jimmy Wales and John Mackey, they create the conditions in which people can effectively self-organize their work rather than assembling a cadre of bosses to micromanage every aspect of a rigid, predetermined plan.

Facilitative leaders understand that power with people is far more effective than power over people, especially in twenty-first-century business. That's because one of the consequences of the Digital Revolution is that the locus of power has shifted from "being in charge" to "being connected." Facilitative leaders don't exert influence by expanding their span of control; rather, they lead by aggregating collective intelligence and expanding shared understanding across all the workers within the organization. Thus, they behave very differently in engaging their fellow workers.

Facilitative leaders operate from the knowledge that nobody is smarter than everybody. They would rarely, if ever, substitute their own judgments for the collective judgment of a diverse group of knowledgeable coworkers. Instead, they bring people together and facilitate creative meetings. For example, if there are more than ten people in a meeting, they might divide into smaller groups of five or six people to get the benefit of different perspectives and to ensure that more people participate in the sharing of ideas. As the group's facilitator, they don't participate in any of these discussions because their role is to remain neutral and to be a steward for the aggregation of the thinking that emerges from the small groups.

Facilitative leaders also make it safe and even invite people to express dissent from the traditional or acceptable ways. Imagine how very different the outcome might have been if the recording industry had been in the hands of facilitative leaders. Surely, there were workers inside the industry who knew the future of music was in digital downloads. If the industry had had leaders with the ability to access the collective wisdom of its own workers, those leaders might have pursued a very different strategy by acquiring Napster, and perhaps we would all be buying our music from the new Napster rather than from Apple's iTunes!

The facilitative leader appreciates that when power is about being connected, you lead by consensus, not by command. The executives at Verizon learned this lesson in the spring of 2012 when they tried to introduce a $2 fee for people who paid their bills online. The executives were forced within twenty-four hours to rescind the fee because the consensus among their well-connected customers was overwhelmingly opposed to the misguided charge.

While traditional managers may scoff at the notion of management by consensus, an increasingly hyper-connected world is, nevertheless, steadily rendering management-by-command obsolete. That's why leaders need to change their personal stance. If they become skilled in the practice of facilitation, they will tap into the power that drives the extraordinary success of companies like Wikipedia, Linux, Amazon, eBay, and Google.

PRACTICE #14: DETACH FROM OUTCOME. The foundational concept of this practice is that, in solving complex issues, there is no one right solution and not every solution is right. More often than not, there is a set of right solutions, and it is the leader's job to guide the organization in selecting a solution from this set. The probability of selecting one of these solutions is much greater if the leader leverages collective intelligence rather than relying on her own individual intelligence. To do this, the leader needs to detach herself from any particular outcome. Only then will she be sufficiently open to whatever solution emerges from the collective wisdom. This is a lesson that I learned firsthand during a product strategy session that I facilitated when I was an executive with the Blue Cross Blue Shield Federal Employee Program (FEP).

The objective of our strategy session was to design a new health insurance product for our portfolio of offerings as part of a growth strategy to expand into segments of the federal employee market where Blue Cross Blue Shield had historically been weak. The innovative new product would be a lower-priced EPO (Exclusive Provider Option) offering. In exchange for its lower price, the proposed EPO product, while providing generous benefits for using doctors and hospitals in the carrier's network, would not provide any out-of-network benefits.

There were two major challenges to the successful execution of this strategy. First, Blue Cross Blue Shield was not certain that the Office of Personnel Management (OPM), which has responsibility for administering health insurance benefits for federal employees, would agree to an EPO product option. Second, the execution of this new product model would require significant time-challenged modifications to the carrier's claims processing systems that would need to begin well before the well-established annual date that Blue Cross Blue Shield and OPM agree on product options for the next calendar year.

To address these challenges, I had instructed the participants in the strategy session to meet in small group discussions to identify alternative product designs in the event that the employer would not accept an EPO product. I explained that by having an alternative, we could begin systems work on both alternatives until product discussions were concluded, enabling us to complete the systems installation of whichever product alternative was ultimately accepted by OPM. It sounded like a reasonable business plan in view of the fact that the board had already decided that a new product had to be in place for the next benefits year. I was invested in the outcome that being prepared meant having alternative options in case OPM did not accept our preferred product proposal.

However, before we could begin this exercise, one of the participants protested, "We can't do this. It's the wrong thing to do." He went on to explain that we needed to make a commitment to the EPO model and do whatever was necessary to make it happen, even if that meant waiting an additional year to get OPM comfortable with this new product design. He further stated that our existing resources could not support working on two alternative product designs concurrently, and, thus, we could not reasonably expect to do either one before the start of the next benefit year at the level necessary to deliver the expected excellent service.

Despite three attempts on my part to coax the group to define alternatives, the participants continued to push back. While I had the positional authority to force the outcome, I realized that there was something important happening in the room and that I needed to stop fighting it and let it be.

And so I detached myself from outcome and opened up a large group discussion, sharing with the group the pressures I felt to both acknowledge the wisdom of the session participants and to comply with the will of the board.

Over the next hour, a genuine dialogue developed as we together worked the problem of resolving these seemingly irreconcilable positions. As the discussion evolved, one member of the group suggested that we escalate the date for reaching agreement with OPM on the form of the new product option. If that could be done, the new product design would be known before beginning critical systems work and the board's directive would be met. This simple idea was the breakthrough that gave us the outcome we needed. By letting go of my preferred outcome and trusting the wisdom of the assembled crowd, the single hour that it took us to arrive at a workable solution saved countless months of what would have been wasted energy and helped build a new product strategy that did indeed drive the increased market share we desired.

Resetting the Meetings

PRACTICE #15: COLLABORATION SOFTWARE. Collaboration software provides a platform for people involved in a common task to share conversations, documents, files, and other pertinent information so they can pool their knowledge to achieve quicker and more responsive solutions to important business problems. There are a large number of various applications available to meet different collaborative needs.

The most well-known collaboration software tool is the wiki, which is the foundation for Wikipedia's operating system. A wiki is a website that allows its users to comment on and modify one another's text. It is typically used for creating and documenting the development of software or for producing open sourced products. Most wikis allow anonymous editing without the need to have an account with the site, although registered users are often entitled to additional editing functions, as is the case with Wikipedia.

Wikis can support open or closed communities. Open communities allow customers and other people outside the organization to participate in a company's wikis, while participation in closed communities is limited to the employees within the organization. Wikipedia is an example of an open community where literally anyone in the world can participate. The advantage this creates is that Wikipedia's principal product is created by its customers at essentially no cost. In most companies, however, wiki communities are private and are used primarily for the development of in-house systems and applications.

Collaboration software can also support the acceleration of conversations within a company. A popular tool, used by more than 90,000 companies, is Yammer, which is similar in structure to Twitter but is usually restricted to the closed community within the organization.[15] Yammer enables the unrestricted free flow of information and ideas across organizational levels and geographical areas, recognizing that innovative thinking can come from anywhere within the company. The software tool provides people with the ability to ask questions and get timely answers or to conduct a poll and get rapid results.

The most popular use of collaboration software is for content and document management across an enterprise. Almost all *Fortune* 500 companies have an enterprise tool, with more than 75 percent subscribing to Microsoft's SharePoint Web application platform. SharePoint provides companies with a central location for storing electronic documents or images of paper documents. It also allows for the tracking of different versions of documents by different users and often serves as the foundation for corporate knowledge management systems.

PRACTICE #16: LET'S PLAY A GAME. Sometimes when your best work isn't working, the best thing to do is to play a game. That's what Rob McEwen of Goldcorp did when his geologists couldn't find his elusive gold. It's also the solution Firas Khatib employed when he turned to the Foldit community to solve the perplexing puzzle behind the workings of the protein-cutting enzyme.

The Digital Revolution has created the unprecedented capacity to access the collective intelligence of the world's brightest people by bringing them together in virtual rooms to help us solve our most vexing problems. Whether sponsoring a contest with monetary prizes or engaging the voluntary efforts of online gamers, Web-based games and contests are highly effective options for many businesses today. Scientific and technological companies searching for breakthroughs in fields such as biogenetics, energy, or pharmacology may have the opportunity to slash R&D budgets by using online games to harness the wisdom of the crowd.

Online games vary in complexity from simple text-based applications to sophisticated virtual worlds populated by communities of passionate players. The games are designed to promote teamwork, where individual players can combine their skills to achieve higher-quality solutions than they could achieve on their own. When diversity, intelligence, and passion are combined to solve a common problem in an environment of free-flowing information, we develop the capacity to accelerate our learning and quickly identify practical solutions to complex problems. Online games, such as Foldit, are proof positive that nobody really is smarter or faster than everybody, once you have the right tools.

PRACTICE #17: THE ELEGANT SET. The Elegant Set demonstrates that aggregating collective intelligence isn't limited to digital applications. Using innovative meeting technology, it is possible to replicate the power of a wiki in face-to-face meetings.

The Elegant Set is a facilitated exercise that is especially useful when an organization is under pressure to deliver a solution or to implement a strategy, and it is caught in a cycle of endless debate driven by deep irreconcilable differences among a large group of key stakeholders.

The facilitator begins the exercise by dividing the large group into smaller groups of seven to ten people and asking each group to identify its five most important concerns on flip charts. After the completion of the small group discussions, a presenter from each group reports the five items and answers any clarifying questions (see Practice #8).

When all the groups have reported, the flip chart pages are taped on one wall of the room with the pages lined up next to each other. The facilitator then asks the group to look over all the flip charts and identify items that may be identical or similar across the different small group reports. As items are identified as similar, the facilitator checks with the individuals from the small groups that reported those items to see if they agree that the items are indeed the same. If the groups agree, the facilitator then checks with the large group as to which item should remain and which should be deleted. Once agreement is reached, the facilitator draws a box around the retained item and draws a line through the deleted item.

When all the items on the flip charts have been condensed into a single list, the facilitator passes out to each individual small strips of stick-on dots with three to five dots per strip. The facilitator asks each person to place her dots next to the items that are most important to her. Each person is free to apply her dots any way that she wants. Thus, for example, if each strip contained four dots, an individual could place four separate dots on four different items, or all four dots on one item, or two dots on one item and two dots on each of two different items, etc. This flexibility in applying dots ensures two things. First, dots are placed on only the most important items. Second, the ability to apply more than one dot to a particular item provides the opportunity for minority points of view to remain a part of the continuing dialogue.

Once all the dots have been applied to the items on the condensed list, the facilitator tallies the votes and observes where the natural "break point" is in the voting results. For example, if forty people voted four dots each on a list of ten items and the voting results were thirty, twenty-nine, twenty-seven, twenty-six, fifteen, fourteen, eight, five, four, and two, then the natural break point would be after the fourth item (i.e., the items getting thirty, twenty-nine, twenty-seven, and twenty-six dots). This means that the top four items would constitute the Elegant Set.

Typically, the Elegant Set contains an element that is key for one of the factions in the group, an apparently contradictory element that's important to a faction with an opposing point of view, and one or two elements that help to bridge the apparently opposing elements such that the set taken as a whole is acceptable to all the stakeholders. The beauty of the Elegant Set exercise is that the process moves a group past endless debate over deep differences by tapping into the collective intelligence of the group to identify workable common ground to move forward.

PRACTICE #18: 25/10 CROWD SOURCING. This exercise comes from a collection of innovative meeting formats known as Liberating Structures. Collated by Keith McCandless and Henri Lipmanowicz, these facilitated meeting formats are innovative ways for engaging and unleashing the power of everyone in shaping the organization's future.

25/10 Crowd Sourcing enables a large group to generate and identify ten bold ideas for action in twenty-five minutes or less. The exercise begins with the facilitator asking each of the members of the group, "If you were ten times bolder, what big idea would you recommend? What first step would you take to get started?" Each of the participants is then given five minutes to write one idea and its first action step on a three by five index card.

After the five minutes, the facilitator asks each participant to quickly find a partner. In their pairs, the participants have two minutes to exchange and score each other's ideas using a five-point scale with 1 being *Does nothing for me* to 5 meaning *Wow! We have to do this.* During the exchange of cards, the participants do not read their own cards aloud; they merely pass their cards to each other. If there is any discussion, it's initiated by the scorer, who might have clarifying questions to get a better understanding of the idea. The scores are then written on the backs of the cards. The exchange and scoring in pairs is repeated for four more rounds with different partners in each of the rounds.

When the five rounds are completed, each participant calculates the sum of the scores on the back of her index card for a total score that should range from 5 to 25. The facilitator then asks, "Who has a score of 25? 24? 23?" and so on, inviting each cardholder to read out the idea and the action step until the top ten ideas/actions are identified.

To learn more, visit the Liberating Structures website: www.liberating structures.com.

PRACTICE #19: WISE CROWDS. Wise Crowds is another exercise from the Liberating Structures collection. This exercise is a way for individuals to ask for and get help immediately from different people with different perspectives. The exercise is conducted in fifteen-minute rounds and works with groups of any size from five to 150 people.

If you're starting with a large group, the facilitator divides it into smaller groups of five to seven people. In forming the small groups, a mixture of people across functions is ideal. For the first fifteen-minute round, one member from each of the small groups volunteers to be a *client*. The remaining members are *consultants*. The client has two minutes to describe the challenge that she needs help with. The consultants then have three minutes to ask clarifying questions. After the clarifying questions are complete, the client turns her back to the group, and the consultants, working as a team, have eight minutes to generate questions, advice, or recommendations. During this time, the client listens but does not participate in the discussion. For the final two minutes, the client turns back to the group and describes what was useful about the experience.

Additional rounds may be conducted as time permits with new clients for each of the different rounds.

This exercise is powerful because it does away with boring briefings and updates; refines skills in giving, receiving, and asking for help; and taps into the collective wisdom of the group by working across silos.

To learn more, visit the Liberating Structures website: www.liberating structures.com.

Resetting the Measures

PRACTICE #20: COLLECTIVE FORECASTS. In early 2005, Jeff Severts, a vice president at Best Buy, became intrigued with the notion that the nonexperts at the company might provide better sales forecasts than the traditional experts. In a retail business, accurate sales forecasts are essential. If forecasts are too high, excess inventory cuts into quarterly earnings; if sales predictions are too low, the company risks lost sales. At Best Buy, it was not uncommon for the expert merchant teams to miss forecasts by as much as 10 percent.[16]

Having recently attended a talk by James Surowiecki on his bestseller, *The Wisdom of Crowds*, Severts decided to try an experiment. In late January, he sent out an e-mail to several hundred Best Buy employees, inviting them to predict gift-card sales for February. To encourage participation, the person making the most accurate estimate would receive a $50 gift card. Severts received 192 replies. In early March, he compared the aggregated prediction from his experiment and the official company forecast with actual sales results. The official forecast was 95 percent accurate while the crowd's forecast was 99.5 percent correct.

In August 2005, Severts tested his experiment on the larger challenge of companywide sales for the upcoming holiday season, increasing the prize to a $100 gift card. This time, more than 350 people submitted sales estimates. In early January 2006, when the final sales were tallied, the merchant experts' forecast was 93 percent accurate and the crowd's estimate was, amazingly, 99.9 percent correct.

There are times when diversity trumps ability. In the retail business, having the capacity to formulate collective forecasts can pay dividends in the improvement of quarterly earnings.

PRACTICE #21: CONSENSUS HIGH PERFORMERS. One of the dangers of the traditional supervisor–subordinate relationship is that organizations unwittingly work against collaboration by tying performance and compensation to serving the needs of a single supervisor. A practice that we used at Blue Cross Blue Shield FEP to guard against this dynamic and to promote a collaborative culture was Consensus High Performers.

Each year, as part of our annual performance review discipline, the senior leadership team would discuss the proposed high performers among the 150 people in our central office. High performers received significantly more compensation than employees who were designated as competent performers. Each member of the senior team would propose candidates for high performance from their areas, and the team would discuss the merits of the recommendation. Only those candidates who received the consensus agreement of the whole leadership team would be awarded the designation of high performer and its increased compensation opportunity.

This qualitative measure of performance sent a clear message that pleasing the boss was not sufficient for succeeding in our organization. In a collaborative culture, people need to approach one another as mutual customers and make it their jobs to understand what is most important to their colleagues. Nothing breaks down silos more effectively than turning the workplace into a community of mutual customers.

CHAPTER SUMMARY: KEY POINTS

→ One of the consequences of the Digital Revolution is that the locus of power has shifted from "being in charge" to "being connected." Executive power no longer comes from dominating the thinking or directing the work of others. It now comes from integrating the best of everyone's ideas and leveraging platforms of mass collaboration.

→ When technological advances make networks smarter and faster than hierarchies, self-organizing teams of workers with diversified skills consistently outperform those whose work is organized and directed by persons in authority.

→ The more voices you can get into the same room at the same time, the better the knowledge and the faster you can transform that knowledge into execution—provided that you have workable collective learning processes.

→ When you have the capability to aggregate and leverage collective intelligence, you discover that there are many times when diversity trumps ability.

→ Knowledge is an abundant and not a scarce resource; the only way it grows is by giving it away.

6

Build Shared Understanding
by Bringing Everyone Together
in Open Conversations

The Blue Cross Blue Shield Federal Employee Program (FEP) is a business alliance of the thirty-eight independent Blue Cross and Blue Shield carriers, which collectively provides healthcare coverage for 4.6 million federal employees and their family members across the United States. FEP is a unique business alliance, unlike almost any other business organization. The best analogy to describe how it works comes from an offhand comment made several years ago by a management consultant FEP had hired, who remarked that the only other organization he had worked with that was similar to FEP was the National Football League.

Just as each of the teams in the NFL is a separate business organization with its own ownership and management, each of the Blue Cross Blue Shield plans has a separate board and management group. Whereas the NFL has a commissioner's office to provide the general management for the league, FEP has a director's office to coordinate the joint efforts of the health insurance alliance. Another similarity between the NFL and FEP is that, given the limited options to centrally manage a large number of independent companies, the management challenge of each of these business alliances can be best described as "herding cats."

In 2006, the federal government decided to supplement the health insurance program that it had offered since 1960 with separate programs to provide dental and vision benefits for federal workers. At the time, I was the chief executive of the FEP director's office, and we took the lead in helping design the products that the Blue Plans proposed to offer as part of the new benefits program. While we were working on the dental product, a difficult issue emerged that almost derailed the Blue Plans' ability to put forward a dental offering. The particular sticking point involved the design of a new insurance claims processing model to coordinate benefits between the central processor of the existing FEP health insurance product and the central processor for the new proposed dental insurance product. The health product central processor and the dental product central processor each proposed very different processing models, and each processor passionately advocated its model. Because of speed-to-market requirements, selection of one of these models was critical to moving the project forward. However, given the decentralized nature of the business alliance, a command decision by the FEP director's office was not a practical option. The only decision that would work was one that all parties could support.

Rather than trying to resolve the issue through traditional negotiation or debate, we used an innovative meeting format known as Work-Thru to constructively facilitate closure of the contentious issue. A Work-Thru (as discussed in Chapter 3) is a facilitated meeting that gathers representatives from all areas involved in a project or initiative whole system in one place to leverage the group's collective intelligence to quickly resolve complex or difficult issues. (Some of the practices used in a Work-Thru, such as Clarifying Questions, the Elegant Set, Rotating Tables, and Milestone Timelines are described in this book.)

As the Work-Thru meeting approached, many of the invited participants were skeptical about whether a timely consensus on a model could be reached, and they were dreading the tense and difficult conversations they anticipated. On meeting day, recognizing the importance of our selection and the passionate advocacy of both central processors, I invited each of the processors to open the meeting with a presentation of its proposed model. Each presentation was delivered without interruption, and a period of clarifying questions followed. After that, I divided the thirty-five participants into four small table groups and asked each group to select one of the two models and to list the top three to four reasons for that selection. Following forty-five minutes in the small group discussions, each table reported its results with all four tables selecting the health product processor's model for reasons that were obviously consistent across the four groups.

When all the small group reports were complete, I observed that it appeared from the table reports that there was a clear consensus for using the health processor's model. Everyone in the room nodded in apparent agreement. To be absolutely sure that true consensus and agreement had been reached, I asked the participants, "Is there anyone in the room who cannot live with this selection?" I cautioned the group that no one should agree just for the sake of going along, nor should anyone hang on to a preference just for the sake of not giving up on his personal druthers. Rather, if there was any individual—even one person—who truly believed the selected approach would fail and thus could not live with the selection, then that individual needed to come forward and the group needed to stay with the discussion. There are times when one person sees something that the rest of the group does not, and that insight might very well move the group in a different direction. Consensus is not about the majority ruling; rather, it's about identifying the optimal workable solution that everyone can live with.

In response to this final question, all thirty-five participants—including those who initially advocated the model that was not selected—agreed that they could live with and support the chosen model. With true consensus and agreement achieved, the project could move forward. Because we took the time to gather the whole system in one place and had the ability to access and leverage the group's collective intelligence, we were able to craft an effective shared understanding that was far more powerful than a negotiated agreement or a command decision would have been. Everyone was involved in the decision, no one left the room feeling unheard, and, best of all, we were able to "herd cats" by accomplishing real closure on a contentious issue in only ninety minutes.

SHARED UNDERSTANDING OVER COMPLIANCE

As FEP's chief executive, I had the authority to make the decision about which processing model to use. However, I chose not to exercise that authority because experience had taught me that building shared understanding produces far better performance than demanding compliance.

Shared understanding is the elixir of Wiki Management and the organizational force that drives extraordinary performance. When all workers understand how their individual contributions fit together and how those contributions create value that truly delights customers, they become highly engaged. In high engagement environments, everyone understands what everyone else is doing. As a positive consequence, people naturally recognize problems and issues as they arise, and they know whom to involve at the first sign of trouble so that small problems don't fester and become large breakdowns.

In traditional organizations where compliance is the primary vehicle for execution, people are rewarded for performing isolated tasks. They learn quickly to respect the chain of command, watch what they say, keep out of other people's business, and, most importantly, stick to their own jobs. A clear indicator of a high compliance environment is the all too familiar phrase, "That's not my job."

The problem with high compliance environments is that no one knows what everyone else is doing, and as a consequence, a pervasive problem that clouds an increasing number of workplaces is that most people come to work feeling nobody—sometimes including themselves—knows what they are doing. The definition of disengagement is workers who have a deep sense of organizational isolation because they don't understand how their contributions fit together with others. This isolation becomes even more pronounced when the rest of the world is increasingly hyper-connected.

The antidote for disengagement is actually rather simple: Create an environment in which everyone knows what everyone else is doing. And the best way to create a high engagement environment is to use shared understanding rather than compliance as the primary driver of execution.

The first rule of shared understanding is that the understanding is shared and not mandated. That is why so many corporate mission statements become nothing more than meaningless, nice-sounding intentions. In Wiki Management organizations, leaders don't promulgate what's most important to the company. Instead, they collaborate with their workers in forums of cross-functional teams where the participants are invited to speak candidly, where all voices are heard equally, where anyone is free to agree or disagree without political repercussions, where managers and workers are jointly accountable to each other, and where consensus about the company's mission is achieved through innovative social processes that promote dialogue and the rapid integration of the best of everyone's thinking.

Shared understanding is real only when it is built from the thoughts and voices of everyone in the organization. It emerges from the interplay of the observations and the ideas of all who are involved in delivering value to customers. When worker knowledge is comingled with customer and company values to create a shared understanding of how the company makes a difference in the lives of its customers, then workers are able to help the company master accelerating change by being empowered to make real-time decisions in the face of continuous change.

EMERGENT OVER DIRECTED

While the notion of building shared understanding is emotionally compelling and conceptually simple, it's difficult for many managers to put into practice. That's because shared understanding is something that emerges rather than something that's directed. Traditional managers have little experience in leading emergent processes, which generally look chaotic at the beginning. They are more skilled in giving directions and setting up mechanisms to maintain order across their projects or departments. Order is a prime value for traditional managers because it's tangible evidence that the managers are clearly in charge and on top of their work. Most managers are uncomfortable with chaos and do everything they can to eliminate the demon whenever it appears. However, if today's managers want to master the challenges presented by the unprecedented combination of accelerating change, escalating complexity, and ubiquitous connectivity, they will need to change how they value both order and chaos.

When companies have difficulty with change, you are likely to find that they have a very low tolerance for chaos and a high need to preserve the established order. This is problematic in fast-changing times because change always entails the emergence of a new order, and this new order inevitably creates a certain amount of chaos. In times of great change, the most successful managers are those who understand that chaos isn't something to be avoided—it's something to be worked through.

When you think about it, every project has two phases: order and chaos. Our only choice as managers is the sequence. In the typical command-and-control organization, when faced with complexity and confusion, chaos is rarely embraced. The tendency is to choose order by coming up with an immediate plan, organizing resources, designating an accountable leader, and setting up a periodic reporting structure. In other words, when confronted with the anxiety of the unknown, the usual reaction of traditional managers is to embrace the basic activities of the hierarchical management model: planning, organizing, directing, coordinating, and controlling. But all too often, this premature embrace of order is actually counterproductive, leading eventually to chaos in the later stages of projects and resulting in significant cost overruns and delays, if not outright failure, and the ensuing disengagement of the workers.

When order is embraced prematurely, managers deny themselves the opportunity to discover what is most important at the start of complex and difficult projects: to discover what they don't know that they don't know. These are the important factors that are outside our awareness at the beginning of initiatives and that inevitably come back to bite us, sometimes fatally, at the end of projects.

When managers feel overwhelmed by confusion and chaos in confronting an important and complex issue, this is a sure sign that they are at a place where they don't know what they don't know. If managers are to break through this confusion, they need to embrace rather than avoid the chaos and discover the key questions that need to be addressed so that they can become aware of everything they need to know at the start of the project. In embracing the chaos, they need to think creatively by detaching from predetermined outcomes and leading cross-functional teams in a facilitated inquiry. They also need to trust the power of serendipity and prepare to be surprised when they uncover what they don't know that they don't know.

GOOD SURPRISES AND BAD SURPRISES

Creativity cannot be planned; it can only be facilitated. This is why large traditional organizations have so much difficulty with creativity. The centralized planning that's pervasive in command-and-control organizations is designed to eliminate surprises and therefore blunts serendipity. In this approach, unfortunately, the only surprises that centralized planning seems to eliminate are the "good surprises." Far too often, the dysfunctional silo structures of hierarchical organizations inadvertently lead to "bad surprises" in the later stages of complex projects.

Good surprises are the breakthroughs and alternative ways of thinking that result in cost or time reductions, operational efficiencies, product innovations, or new business opportunities. More often than not, good surprises are discovered by entrepreneurs who are not saddled with the controlling infrastructures of traditional organizations. Bad surprises are the unintended consequences of centralized planning in rigid bureaucratic structures when things do not come together at the end as planned because different parts of the bureaucracy had different understandings or—worse yet—different agendas.

Surprises in organizations are like cholesterol in the human body. Just as an abundance of bad cholesterol and a low amount of good cholesterol can lead to cardiac arrest, an abundance of bad surprises and the absence of good surprises can lead to significant business failure. Likewise, as the body needs good cholesterol for sustained health, organizations need good surprises for sustained business success. This is especially important in fast-changing times because good surprises can greatly improve established organizations' capacity to keep up with entrepreneurs, compete with new players, or leverage the power of an existing brand into new markets. In the wiki world, companies that desire long-term sustainable growth must have the capacity to invite and facilitate good surprises and to quickly convert and execute those good surprises into business results. Given the pace of change in business today, this is not an option but rather a required competency.

When managers are skilled in leading emergent processes, they have the wherewithal to uncover the true order in the chaos. They are able to facilitate identifying elegant solutions to complex issues that often turn out to be relatively simple once the right elements are put together. This discovery of true order does two things. First, it creates a powerful shared understanding among the cross-functional team that created the breakthrough. Second, the simple elegance of the solution translates very effectively to both decision makers and workers outside the team, leading to quick adoption of the solution and an even broader shared understanding to drive extraordinary performance throughout the organization. The simplicity and the clarity of a meaningful shared understanding that emerges from the collective intelligence of cross-functional teams goes a long way to producing good surprises early on in a project and to minimizing or even eliminating bad surprises in the final hours of the work effort.

PRACTICES

The following are actual practices used by companies to build shared understanding by bringing everyone together in open conversations. Given your role within your organization and the current state of your corporate culture, some practices may work better than others. Focus on the two or three practices that would best work in your particular business circumstances.

Resetting the Managers

PRACTICE #22: MANAGE THE CONTAINER. Before the mid-1990s, writing the content of computer programs involved far more work than necessary because software specialists didn't have a practical way to share their methods. A significant amount of programming is generic and nonproprietary, and a substantial chunk of time could be saved if programmers could pool their nonproprietary routines and focus on the unique proprietary aspects of their software development. In early 1995, Ward Cunningham came up with an innovative solution for how programmers could share their common staples when he launched the WikiWikiWeb site.[1]

In creating the "wiki," as it came to be known among its early aficionados, Cunningham constructed a container in which programmers could effectively self-organize their work. The breakthrough concept behind Cunningham's innovation was the then radical practice of allowing any coder to edit any page on the site. Thus, the management of content became the responsibility of the users rather than the managers. This radical concept of content self-management has revolutionized the management of technology by providing the foundation for the growing open source industry as well as the impetus for rapid rise in the Agile approach to software development.

Open source leaders and Agile managers don't manage content—they manage the container. The container is the virtual or the physical space in which people work together.

When managers orchestrate the content of work, they prescribe both the what and the how of the work to be done and usually exercise tight control over the production efforts. Unfortunately, centrally controlled review processes can dramatically slow work down, as Jimmy Wales and Larry Sanger discovered when the initial iteration of their online encyclopedia, Nupedia, could produce only twenty-five articles in its first year.

On the other hand, when managers orchestrate the container of work, they facilitate what needs to be done by providing a simple structure to guide workers in the self-organization of how to produce results. Although it may appear counterintuitive, managing the container is a far more productive strategy than managing the content and usually leads to significantly higher levels of performance. Thus, when Wales and Sanger embraced Cunningham's wiki, renamed their start-up Wikipedia, and shifted their focus from managing the content to managing the container, they made an incredible leap to extraordinary performance.

While Wikipedia is an example of how to manage a virtual container, Agile software developers have used similar principles to manage better meetings in producing their work efforts. By breaking large projects into smaller three- or four-week mini-projects, called sprints, they frequently gather all key players in one room to inspect and adapt their work deliverables to ensure alignment with customer values, as well as to learn quickly what's working, what's not working, and what needs to be done before the end of the next sprint. These sprint meetings are usually led by a facilitator whose role is to manage the container of the meeting rather than to actively participate in the content of the discussion. The facilitator manages the time spent on topics, ensuring that the group does not get bogged down on minutiae. He also makes sure that all voices are heard and balanced and key points are captured, and he always has a supply of stick-on dots for voting when the group needs to move to consensus. But most importantly, the facilitator is a leader who does not express his opinion and is not invested in a particular outcome. As the group's leader, the facilitator's job is to guide the group in aggregating its collective intelligence and in identifying its own conclusions.

The idea that managers sometimes serve as facilitators who do not express their own opinions and who do not exert influence toward specific outcomes flies in the face of the assumptions of command-and-control management. In traditional meetings, where idea generation tends to be intertwined with decision making, managers are expected to manage the content by taking charge and exerting influence over outcomes. However, when managers focus on managing the container, they understand that their primary role is not to exert influence over the group's thinking but rather to create and to nurture the space in which the group can discover and then leverage its own collective wisdom.

PRACTICE #23: LEADERSHIP TEAM GUESTS. Sometimes the most important information is outside the purview of the leadership team. Whether the team is the C-Suite, an operating council, or a project team, as the pace of change continues to accelerate, there is an increasing risk that everything a team needs to know to make informed decisions is not contained within the group. Clearly, the managers in the recording industry did not have all the information they needed when they pursued a flawed strategy to fight rather than to embrace digital downloading. Imagine how different the result might have been if the managers had invited a few of their millennial employees to join their strategic discussions and had seriously listened to advice from this unusual source.

The practice of Leadership Team Guests is a way to ensure that managers have access to all the critical information they need to make the best decisions. In addition to the usual permanent members, the team is augmented on a rotating basis by two or three individuals from either other levels or other areas within the organization. These guests serve as full members of the team for a fixed period of time—perhaps three or six months—and are selected primarily for the diverse perspectives they can bring to the team. Thus, in a business where the primary customers are young people, inviting young, junior members to participate on a senior-level team could provide a powerful competitive advantage in setting strategy for the company. One of the primary reasons the recording industry failed to innovate its business strategy is that its older boomer decision makers failed to understand the changing values of their much younger customers. That wouldn't have happened if millennial guests had been on the team that decided the strategy.

In addition to expanding the diversity of thinking on the leadership team, inviting guests onto the team takes some of the mystique out of the team's proceedings by providing an effective conduit between the leaders and the workers. This helps prevent the "ivory tower" syndrome that plagues many traditional companies and provides another vehicle for building shared understanding throughout the business. Finally, the practice of Leadership Team Guests provides an opportunity for the team to see its future leadership talent in action, which may be very valuable when it comes time to fill full-time openings on the team.

Resetting the Meetings

PRACTICE #24: SIT BY PROJECT. Valve is a video gaming company based in Bellevue, Washington. Founded in 1996 by former Microsoft employees Gabe Newell and Mike Harrington, the entertainment company prides itself as a center of innovation in a rapidly evolving industry. Valve is designed to maximize creativity and serendipity, and thus the company has no managers and no hierarchy, and every desk is a mobile workstation.

There are no work assignments at the gaming company. Each of the approximately 250 workers is free to choose what projects to work on. Workers aren't assigned to predetermined teams or departments. They work on projects as long as they are making a contribution or until the project is complete. When it's time to move on, each worker is responsible for starting or finding another project. Because their desks have wheels, it's quite easy for Valve staff members to move their workstations to another part of the office space to join their new teams.

At Valve, the primary work unit is the project. Sitting by Project enables an informal, continuous dialogue among workers with a diversity of perspectives. The unusual connections that sometimes occur when seemingly unrelated observations are put together is the root of the serendipity that leads to creative breakthroughs.

If you want to build shared understanding among the members of a critical project team, move them away from their departments and have them physically sit together in a common space. For example, people from sales and marketing would sit with software programmers and engineers. If the members of a critical team continue to sit only with their department colleagues, the opportunity for serendipity is greatly diminished, and the parochial understandings of functional departments are likely to prevail over the best interests of the company. The practice of Sitting by Project is one of the simplest ways to enable the spontaneous building of shared understanding across diverse functional perspectives.

PRACTICE #25: OPEN SPACE MEETINGS. In the mid-1980s, the management consultant Harrison Owen created a highly innovative meeting format that was completely contradictory to almost every principle for how to run an effective meeting. The conventional wisdom is that the best meetings are those with a clear agenda, predetermined time frames, well-prepared speakers, and a strong chairperson to move the group along. Unfortunately, while these well-scripted events may appear to proceed smoothly, the preset agenda can sometimes get in the way of meaningful discussion, and, as a result, there is little passion or shared understanding about what happens after the meeting.

Owen wanted to create a way to hold meetings that tapped into the passions of and fueled a sense of responsibility among the participants. His solution was the Open Space meeting. In Open Space meetings, there are no speakers or presenters, nor is there a predetermined agenda. Instead, the meeting begins with people sitting in a circle, where they formulate the agenda on the spot. Everyone in the room is invited to propose agenda topics by writing the issues and names on a piece of paper at a small table in the middle of the room and then posting the proposed topics on the wall. The topics are then divided into two sessions, with half the topics to be discussed in the first session and the remaining topics to be discussed in the second session.

When each session begins, discussion groups are formed around each topic, and the participants are free to choose the particular discussions that most interest them. If, however, individuals find upon joining a discussion that they are losing interest or not contributing, they are encouraged to follow the one law of Open Space—the "Law of Two Feet"—and go join another discussion group.[2] What happens in the discussions and what actions follow the sessions are the responsibility of the people who join the various groups. For example, in using Open Space as the primary format for our quarterly management meetings at Blue Cross Blue Shield FEP, sometimes the result of the meeting was a good discussion in which people felt fully informed about an important concern. Other times, initiatives were created in the sessions and the participants took responsibility for executing the follow-up plan, as happened when a group created and implemented a very useful job rotation program.

At the end of both sessions, the whole group reconvenes for a sharing of the most important contributions in the group discussions. Rather than receiving a report from each of the discussions, individuals are invited to share only those things that would be most useful to the whole group. For example, a key insight, an innovative discovery, or a lesson learned would be reported. Any actions a group decides to take as a result of the sessions would also be reported, in case others who were not part of that particular discussion would like to volunteer to help.

While the spontaneous nature of this meeting format may contradict everything we've been taught about structuring good meetings, Open Space is a powerful tool and is especially useful when beginning large, complex projects, or as the basic format for periodic management meetings, as we did at FEP. Prior to using Open Space, FEP's quarterly management meetings were a form of death-by-PowerPoint, where all the presenters were more interested in looking good than in having deep discussions of critical issues. When we shifted to the Open Space format, the meetings became more productive, the follow-through efforts were more meaningful, and the managers were far more engaged.

Any manager can facilitate an Open Space session because it requires minimum facilitation skills. The facilitator's responsibilities are (1) to open the session by inviting the participants to write out their agenda items, (2) to organize the topics into two sessions, (3) to announce the start and finish of each of the two sessions, and (4) to bring the group back together after the two sessions for sharing the most important contributions in the small group discussions. While Open Space may not fit all business circumstances, it is a valuable tool for managers interested in promoting high engagement and building shared understanding. You can learn more about Open Space in Harrison Owen's book *Expanding Our Now: The Story of Open Space Technology.*

PRACTICE #26: TOWN HALL CONFERENCE CALLS. The practice of Town Hall Conference Calls was used at Blue Cross Blue Shield FEP to get everyone in the same space at the same time when people working on a common project were geographically distributed across the country.

An effective application of this practice involved the installation of a new claims processing system throughout 2002.

In the health insurance industry, the claims processing system is the operational core of the business. With continual developments in the world of systems technology, health insurers need to overhaul and replace their claims systems every ten to fifteen years. FEP's previous systems replacement in 1985 had not gone smoothly and had been fraught with several major problems, and it took almost a full year to solve all the issues before the system was fully functional. Installing a new system at FEP is a particular challenge because, as previously stated, the business is an alliance of all the independent Blue Cross and Blue Shield Plans, which meant, at the time, that replacing the system was not one installation but rather forty separate installations at each of the then thirty-nine Plans and the national Operations Center.

As we approached this challenge, we not only wanted to avoid the difficulties we had encountered in the 1985 installation, but we also had to stay on budget because of the requirements under our contract with the federal government. We knew this was an enormous task because our outside systems consultants had advised us that the failure rate for new computer systems across all industries was about 50 percent and that cost overruns were more the norm than the exception. Because we had to ensure that the system didn't fail and we had to stay on budget, we began to use the Town Hall Conference Calls as our primary communications channel during the installation of the new system.

The two-hour conference calls were held every week and were open to anyone in the Blue Cross and Blue Shield organizations who worked with FEP. The calls were forums for updates, problem solving, and the sharing of best practices. These facilitated conversations were open and candid, and when word spread of the real progress we were making with the calls, a surprising and unexpected result happened that catapulted the quality of our work to another level: Both the business and the systems staffs began showing up on the calls.

When we first put the weekly calls in place, we had intended them for the systems staff at the various Blue Plans throughout the United States. When the business staff began participating in the calls, we realized that we had stumbled onto a way to effectively bring both the systems people and the business people together in the same space. The benefits of this regular cross-fertilization were immediate and powerful. Because systems requirements—like everything else in fast-changing times—keep evolving, continual connection between the systems designers and the end users is essential if systems initiatives are to succeed. When you meet in two-hour conference calls in open conversations every week, a community of systems and business partners starts to form, and the participants begin to find each other off-line when issues arise. The shared understanding that evolved over the course of these conference calls drove a level of consistent execution that clearly exceeded our expectations. When we threw the switch on the new system on January 1, 2003, not only did the system work as designed, but it came in under budget as well.

PRACTICE #27: TGIF. At 4:30 PM every Friday afternoon, Google employees on the Mountain View, California, campus assemble at the Googleplex café for what they call TGIF. Google workers in other offices around the world are welcome to participate in these weekly gatherings via webcast.[3] Google's founders, Larry Page and Sergey Brin, and its executive chairman, Eric Schmidt, serve as the hosts for these all-hands meetings, where they introduce new hires, summarize the week's key milestones, review the latest financial results, discuss any pending deals, and lead an open-mike question-and-answer session.

TGIF is one of the ways that Google builds shared understanding by bringing everyone together in open conversations. In contrast to typical corporate gatherings, these sessions are low on scripting and high on candor. The highlight of TGIF is the no-holds-barred Q & A. All employees are encouraged to submit questions online and to rate the proposed inquiries using an internal program that identifies the most popular questions.[4]

Regardless of the difficulty of the questions, the three Google leaders handle all questions seriously, honestly, and directly. When leaders are committed to building shared understanding, nothing is not speakable when everyone is gathered together.

TGIF is a practice that any manager or group of managers can put in place. A weekly discipline of meaningful updates, honest inquiry, and candid dialogue is a highly effective way to make sure that everyone's voice is heard, that everybody is connected to what is most important in steering the business, and, most importantly, that the whole team is fully engaged because members understand why their work matters and how their efforts make a difference in the lives of their customers.

PRACTICE #28: FREE MEALS. Another practice that Google uses to create shared understanding is providing free meals for all its employees. While implementing this practice may not be possible for many managers because of budget constraints, it is still worth mentioning to highlight the underlying thinking behind the practice.

The primary reason that Google provides free meals on its campuses is not to offer a competitive employee perk but rather to facilitate a constant companywide conversation.[5] The leaders at Google want their employees to spend as much time as possible on their campuses because they understand that all conversations, whether formal or informal, are valuable. Any conversation is an opportunity for serendipity, a key driver of innovation. At Goggle there is no prohibition against what more traditional companies call socializing because innovative ideas can emerge as easily over lunch as they can in a regular business meeting. For example, as we discussed in Chapter 5, the breakthrough idea for Wikipedia happened over a dinner between two good friends.

Rather than have their people leave the office to go to lunch, Google's managers prefer to encourage workers to gather in a common space where they can socialize with employees with whom they don't usually work. In these chance encounters, they are likely to connect seemingly unrelated ideas as they talk about their diverse interests and activities. Innovation is an inherently social process, and there is perhaps no more meaningful social encounter than people sharing a meal together. This may explain why one of the first moves the former Google executive Marissa Mayer made when she became Yahoo's CEO was to implement the practice of free meals.[6]

Another company that provides free meals is Zappos. Like Google, Zappos doesn't use the practice as a compensation or retention strategy but rather as a way to create a sense of community among employees. The leaders at Zappos are very explicit about their belief that socializing is a key ingredient of their business culture.[7]

While most managers may not have the authority or the budget to implement free meals, they can look for innovative ways to apply the thinking behind the practice. It might be possible to find the budget to facilitate off-work activities such as barbecues at managers' homes, a weekly "happy hour" at a club near the office, or a monthly bowling night. These simple social activities may provide ample opportunities for any company to tap into the power of serendipity.

Resetting the Measures

PRACTICE #29: TEACH THE NUMBERS. When managers recognize that they have to change how they manage to keep up with fast-changing times, many of them start by opening their books to their employees and teaching them the numbers. They believe if they can get workers to shift from thinking like employees to thinking like owners, there will be a significant shift in the way the workers behave. When this shift happens, everyone, not just the managers, feels responsible for the business.

Rick Whitsell, the CEO of Fresno First Bank, understands the power of this behavioral change. Fresno First, a small community bank in central

California, was in its fourth year of operation when the financial crisis of 2008 hit hard. Year four is usually when a community bank breaks even. Unfortunately, the 2008 downturn left Fresno First with a $2.2 million loss.

Whitsell and his board quickly recognized that they were in unchartered waters and needed to manage very differently. The bank's managers made a bold move and decided to open the books to their employees, teach everyone how to read financial statements, and create a line of sight between everyone's job and business success by highlighting the most critical numbers in the statements. Whitsell instituted weekly all-hands meetings where everyone in the bank would come together to share key financial information, collaborate on pressing issues, and create future forecasts by tapping into their collective knowledge.

By involving employees in processing and understanding the bank's numbers and treating his workers as partners rather than subordinates, Whitsell made a commitment to building shared understanding rather than relying on top-down directives. This created an engaged team that enabled Fresno First to make a great leap in its business performance. In 2009, the bank booked a gain of $350,000, and it has realized profits in each of the following years, including a gain of $909,000 in 2012. That's pretty impressive for a young community bank coming of age in the Great Recession.

PRACTICE #30: COLLEAGUE LETTERS OF UNDERSTANDING. Morning Star is a 400-person company where there are no supervisors. The Northern California company is an organization of self-managing professionals who initiate and coordinate their activities with colleagues, customers, and suppliers without any direction from others. With more than $700 million in annual revenues, Morning Star is the world's largest tomato processor.[8] If there are no managers, you may be wondering, how does anything get done? How can a complex manufacturing business with multiple operating processes be so successful if all work is self-managed? The answer is a simple measurement discipline that Morning

Star uses in each of its business units to facilitate the building of shared understanding: the Colleague Letter of Understanding (CLOU).

Before the beginning of each business year, colleagues in each business unit gather to discuss business strategy for the upcoming year. Following these strategic sessions, each worker negotiates a CLOU with the associates he works with or services most directly. Typically, a worker coordinates with about ten colleagues in negotiating a CLOU, and a completed CLOU can list up to thirty specific deliverables with relevant performance metrics.[9] The negotiation and the documented agreement of measurable deliverables form the basis of the shared understanding that directs the coordination of the individual efforts of each of the workers. By holding colleagues accountable to each other rather than to supervisors, Morning Star creates an environment in which everyone becomes each other's customer.

Throughout the year, detailed business information is updated twice a month and made available to all employees so they can track the metrics in their own and their colleagues' CLOUs.[10] The transparency of critical financial and operational data is essential for self-management to work well. Unless people have real-time access to data throughout the year, negotiating CLOUs runs the risk of becoming nothing more than an empty exercise. With the data, CLOUs can be a lever that drives extraordinary business performance.

Although Morning Star uses CLOUs as a substitute for formal supervisors, companies with supervisors might consider using this practice to negotiate some of the performance metrics in their annual appraisal process. Mutually negotiated metrics that reflect a shared understanding among individuals who need to work effectively together can be a powerful tool for improving performance in any organization.

PRACTICE #31: CROSS-FUNCTIONAL GOALS. Cross-functional goals was a practice that we began to use at Blue Cross Blue Shield FEP to correct a serious flaw in our performance evaluation system. Because performance goals were not coordinated across departments, there were many instances where individuals reporting to different supervisors were working on the same project but with different metrics to define success. In other words, our individual performance goals were nothing more than ad hoc collections of uncoordinated and misaligned expectations of functional supervisors who did not share a common perspective. This meant that everyone working on the same initiative was not necessarily working toward the same goal. Obviously, we did not have a performance system that supported the level of collaboration that we needed to effectively lead a business alliance of thirty-nine independent organizations. Our solution was to construct cross-functional goals.

Before the beginning of each business year, a diverse team of managers and workers would gather in a series of meetings to identify the most important cross-functional goals and to propose the common metrics for the measurement of those objectives. The leader of this team would periodically meet with the senior leadership group to review and discuss the developing metrics proposal. Through a series of iterative discussions over several weeks, we would refine the goals and the measures until both the cross-functional and the senior leadership teams reached a consensus. Once common agreement was achieved, the only measures that could be used for the cross-functional goals in individual performance evaluations were the consensus metrics. Supervisors had no discretion over nor could they modify the metrics of the cross-functional goals. This way, we ensured that everyone working on the same project was working toward the same result.

There were four conditions that served as the framework for the construction of our annual cross-functional goals: (1) Only goals that involved at least two departments could be candidates, (2) the determination of the goals and measures was to be achieved through consensus, (3) closure on goals and measures was to be reached before the start of the business year, and (4) all goals and measures had to be either results-based or value-based (see Practice #11).

The consensus practice that we used at FEP to determine cross-functional goals was an important contribution to our transition to becoming a smarter and faster business. This practice encouraged us to collectively examine our evolving market circumstances as we added and deleted goals in response to a changing business environment. The iterative discussions among members of the cross-functional team, the dialogues around the proposed measures with the senior leadership team, and the commitment to determine goals and measures by consensus among all members of both teams reinforced deep collective learning and a powerful shared understanding among our managers and our workers about our most important goals. The common focus around a simple set of cross-functional goals significantly boosted our capacity as effective leaders of the FEP business alliance as, over the five-year period after we installed this practice, we increased our market share by ten percentage points and, year after year, set new records in the operational performance indices across all the Blue Cross Blue Shield organizations in the FEP business alliance.

PRACTICE #32: SOLO/TEAM BALANCED GOALS. In a recent global survey of more than 1,700 chief executive officers, IBM found that collaboration is the number one trait that CEOs are seeking in their employees.[11] More than 75 percent of CEOs see employee collaboration as a key essential for building the connected workforces they need to keep pace with a more connected economy.[12]

If it is true that managers get what they measure, then measuring for collaboration is not an option—it's a critical necessity. Unfortunately, many, if not most, performance evaluation systems measure the performance of individual tasks as the primary means for determining how to allocate limited compensation resources. The typical performance evaluation system is often, unwittingly, an internal competition that pits employee against employee and does little to support meaningful collaboration. Even if collaboration is a factor in the performance tool, it's often a subjective measure rated by a departmental supervisor who's engaged in the same competitive struggle for increased pay. As long as performance focus is on the measurement of individual tasks, a disincentive against collaboration remains.

As managers consider how to redesign measures to incentivize a highly connected workforce, they might be tempted to make all performance metrics team-based goals. However, there's much anecdotal evidence to suggest that when everyone shares equally in the success of the group, some people don't do their fair share of the work and alienate their fellow workers. Evaluating performance exclusively on team-based metrics does not necessarily support collaboration. At FEP, we discovered the best way to incentivize collaboration was to balance both individual and team goals.

The practice of Solo/Team Balanced Goals recognizes that the answer to the riddle of how to construct effective collaboration measures is not an "either/or" choice between individual and team goals, but rather a "both/ and" approach. At FEP, we had six account executives whose primary responsibility was to serve as the single-point liaison with the thirty-nine Blue Cross Blue Shield Plans that participated in our business alliance at the time. Each executive was accountable for the bottom line performance for six or seven Plans. Because the account executives had different professional backgrounds (e.g., finance, operations, or marketing), no single executive had the comprehensive set of skills necessary to address every issue that could arise in one of his Plans. In setting up the performance metrics, we wanted to be sure that each of the account executives would have an incentive to support his colleagues. For example, if an executive with an operations background had a finance problem in one of his Plans, we wanted the executives with a financial background to have an incentive to provide support to help a Plan that wasn't their direct responsibility. A combination of individual and team metrics accomplished the collaboration we desired.

In evaluating their performance, 50 percent of each of the account executive's performance was based on the business metrics of his particular six or seven Plans, and 50 percent was based on the performance of all thirty-nine Plans. This approach ensured that individual accountability was in place for each of the Plans and also supported collaboration because each of the account executives had a stake in the performance of the other Plans. The effectiveness of this approach was evident as the performance of all Plans dramatically increased in the first two years of the practice and then steadily increased each year for the next decade.

CHAPTER SUMMARY: KEY POINTS

→ Consensus is not about the majority ruling. Rather, it's about identifying the optimal workable solution that everyone can live with.

→ The antidote for disengagement is actually rather simple: Create an environment in which everyone knows what everyone else is doing. And the best way to create a high engagement environment is to use shared understanding rather than compliance as the primary driver of execution.

→ In times of great change, the most successful managers are those who understand that chaos isn't something to be avoided. It's something to be worked through.

→ When managers are skilled in leading emergent processes, they have the wherewithal to uncover the true order in the chaos. They are able to identify elegant solutions to complex issues that often turn out to be relatively simple once the right elements are put together.

→ Mutually negotiated metrics that reflect a shared understanding among individuals who need to work effectively together can be a powerful tool for improving performance in any organization.

7

Focus on the Critical Few
Performance Drivers

Major League Baseball has the longest season of any of the professional sports leagues. Each team in both the American League and the National League plays 162 games to determine the five teams from each league that will vie for the titles of League Champions and the chance to play in the World Series for bragging rights as baseball's best team. Making the play-offs is a big deal because performance in sports is about winning championships. Each season, baseball crowns six Division Champions, two League Champions, and one World Series Champion. These teams are baseball's high performers.

Major League Baseball is big business, with more than $7 billion in annual revenues from the seventy-five million fans who fill the stadium seats, the comprehensive network and cable television contracts that broadcast almost every game, and the lucrative merchandising deals for the sale of high-priced team apparel. However, all teams do not have equal resources. In addition to its uniquely long season, another distinguishing characteristic of baseball is that its revenue sharing arrangements are relatively weak compared with those of other sports leagues. As a result, there is a wide diversity in the bottom lines of the thirty individual teams. Teams in large markets, such as New York and Boston, have far greater financial resources than teams in smaller markets, such as Kansas City or San Diego.

The three American League Division Champions in 2012 were the New York Yankees, the Detroit Tigers, and the Oakland Athletics. Given the high annual payrolls of the Yankees and the Tigers at $196 million and $119 million, respectively, it was not surprising that these two power-houses of enviable talent were in the running for baseball's ultimate prize. Less expected was the outstanding performance of the Oakland A's, who, with the lowest payroll in baseball at $49 million, finished the regular season with ninety-four wins and the second best record in the American League, just one win short of the league-leading Yankees. Despite New York dispensing four times the salary dollars paid by the A's, the differ-ence in wins between the teams with the highest and the lowest payrolls in Major League Baseball was a single game.

The management of the Oakland A's is able to do so much more with less because of a thorough understanding of the fourth discipline of Wiki Management: Focus on the critical few performance drivers. The popular film *Moneyball* chronicles the discovery of the innovative strategy used by Billy Beane, the A's general manager, in the 2002 season to turn the finan-cially disadvantaged team into one of baseball's top performers.

For well over a century, the conventional wisdom among baseball managers was that the pathway to building winning teams was to sign star players who excelled in the three metrics of the sport's coveted Triple Crown: batting average, runs batted in, and home runs. Unfortunately, conventional wisdom was of no help to Oakland because Triple Crown contenders command high dollars in the free agent market. There was no way Oakland could compete with a team like the Yankees for the sport's most elite talent. If the A's were going to build a winner, they needed to defy the conventional wisdom and find an alternative pathway.

In rethinking the strategy for building his team, Beane focused on fundamental questions. Which teams go to the postseason? Of course, it's the teams with the most wins. What produces wins? Scoring more runs than your opponent. What produces runs? The answer is simple and obvious: getting on base and advancing around the bases. And, finally, how do players get on base? They get a hit, get hit by a pitch, walk, or reach safely on an error by the defense.

In answering these questions, Beane realized that the conventional wisdom for building teams might not be reliable. While batting average, runs batted in, and home runs are useful indicators of a player's ability to produce runs, they aren't necessarily the best or the most predictive metrics. Batting average, perhaps the most valued of the three traditional measures, is particularly flawed for two reasons. First, it doesn't account for all the ways a batter can get on base. Only hits are factored into the batting average. If a player reaches first base via a walk, an error, or getting hit by a pitch, these instances aren't counted in the average. The second problem with the metric is that all hits are counted the same. Batting average is simply the number of hits divided by the number of at bats. Thus, there is no greater value assigned to a home run than there is to a single.

As Beane contemplated an alternative strategy for building a winning team on his very limited budget, he realized that the most reliable keys to producing runs are getting on base and advancing around the bases. This insight led him to focus on two metrics that were outside the mainstream of baseball talent evaluation: the on-base percentage and the slugging percentage. The on-base percentage counts all the ways that a batter can reach first base, while the slugging percentage gives increasing weight to singles, doubles, triples, and home runs to reflect the statistical reality that a triple or a double is more likely to produce a run than a single.

Beane's strategic rethinking helped him to uncover what are arguably the two most important leading indicators of run production. As a result, he discovered the critical few performance drivers in the sport of baseball.

When Beane ran the numbers using his new metrics, he found, much to his delight, that most of the players with the best statistics were affordable. In fact, many of the players with high on-base or slugging percentages were significantly undervalued by the baseball market. Defying conventional wisdom, Beane took a huge risk and built the 2002 A's roster using these critical few performance drivers as his primary guide. Much to the surprise of baseball's reigning experts, the Oakland A's finished the 2002 season as the American League West Division Champions with a record of 103 wins and 59 losses. Over the next ten years, Beane's innovative approach to recruiting talent would produce three more division championships and three second-place finishes. That's not bad for the team with the lowest payroll in baseball.

LEADING OVER LAGGING

In executing his winning strategy, Beane learned a valuable lesson about measures that applies to any business. All measures are not the same. Some measures are more important than others. In fact, in any project or activity, there are usually a handful of measures that are the key indicators of ultimate success or failure. These measures gauge the few drivers that directly influence or directly correlate with the majority of the remaining measures.

The challenge for organizations is to identify the true drivers of success—you can't just arbitrarily pick any small set of measures. For years, baseball managers tracked the three metrics of the Triple Crown because, in the early days of the sport long before we had computers, these statistics were easy to measure and readily available. But what's easy to measure is not necessarily what's most important to measure. While batting average and home runs are leading indicators, they're not the best measures because these conventional metrics correlate better with individual prowess than team performance. In identifying the on-base and slugging percentages as the critical few drivers of team performance, Beane discovered something that is true for many businesses. The most important lead measures are often already there, but nobody is tracking them because they are either not easy to measure or nobody has made the connection between the new metrics and performance. In the case of baseball, the new metrics were easy to measure thanks to modern computer technology, but until Beane, none of the sport's executives had made the connection.

The identification of the critical few drivers is not as easy as it may appear because the most important leading indicators are not always intuitively obvious, and many times they may actually appear to be counterintuitive. For example, the number of people with Internet access turned out to be a critical leading indicator for the printed encyclopedia business, but because printed encyclopedia executives could not envision themselves as online providers, they were unable to make the connection between the number of online users and their performance. Thus, they unwittingly ceded their business to Wikipedia. Because the encyclopedia executives failed to recognize this counterintuitive metric relationship, they remained focused on monitoring their key lagging indicator: the number of sales of encyclopedia sets. By the time they realized their business model was obsolete, it was too late for them to adapt because Wikipedia had irrevocably disrupted their market.

When companies remain almost exclusively focused on lagging measures, their managers rob themselves of the most important information they need for managing their businesses in fast-changing times. Lagging measures, by definition, provide information about outcomes. The problem with tracking outcomes is that the information provided by these measures is not actionable. If the quarterly earnings are below expectations, there's nothing managers can do to change the result.

A simple yet pervasively misunderstood rule of business is you can't manage results by tracking results. You can manage results only by tracking the drivers of results. This is not to imply that results are not important. Quite the contrary, the achievement of positive results is the goal of business, and managers should continue to be rewarded based on how well they have performed. But if managers want to influence their results, they need to turn their focus to the critical few drivers of performance.

A good leading measure has two basic attributes: It's reliably predictive of achieving desired results, and it is actionable by the managers.[1] Leading indicators let managers know if their expected results are likely to occur. But more important, if it appears that the business is underperforming, leading indicators provide managers with sufficient time to make the right decision between two very different courses of actions: Do they correct or do they adapt?

The problem with using lagging indicators as the primary management tool is that by the time trouble is recognized, managers are likely to find themselves in a full-blown crisis with very limited options. Under the pressure of needing to react quickly, most managers immediately focus on corrective action. This is exactly what happened when the recording industry missed the market shift to digital downloading and myopically focused on its flawed legal strategy to protect its traditional business model. Had the industry been monitoring its most important leading measures, it would have recognized the market shift before album sales began to plummet and could have explored the full range of its strategic options in time enough to better influence its fate. Given the strength of the market shift, it is highly likely that the industry would have chosen adaptive action over corrective action had executives had the time to reflect before being under pressure to act. An adaptive strategy could very well have positioned the traditional industry for a powerful second act based on an innovative business model.

In a business world reshaped by accelerating change, escalating complexity, and ubiquitous connectivity, managers can't afford to manage their businesses by focusing only on the outcome metrics that matter most to the Wall Street analysts. If they want to keep the financial community and their shareholders happy, the more effective path is to focus on the leading indicators that either drive performance or, more important, let the managers know when it's time to make a big shift and adapt to changing customer values. The only way managers can keep the analysts and the shareholders constantly happy is to keep their focus on what's most important to the customers. In the end, shareholder value is dependent upon customer value, and the key to continually delivering customer value is to know the difference between when it's time to make a correction and when it's time to make a change.

PRACTICES

The following are actual practices used by companies to focus on the critical few performance drivers. Given your role within your organization and the current state of your corporate culture, some practices may work better than others. Focus on two or three practices that would best work in your particular business circumstances.

Resetting the Managers

PRACTICE #33: SIMPLE RULES. In Chapter 2, we discussed how, in the wiki world, leaders don't assume that their organizations work like mechanical systems. Instead, they design their enterprises based on the three fundamental organizing principles of complex adaptive systems. One of those principles is that simple rules guide complex collective behavior.

Wikipedia is an example of an organization that uses the practice of Simple Rules to effectively organize a large and complicated business. From the very beginning, Wikipedia has used just four simple rules to guide the complex collective effort of building an online encyclopedia for the planet. The first and most important of these rules is that all articles present a neutral point of view. This means that there can be only one rendition of every article and that proponents of differing factions have to dialogue to form a consensus. As we know only too well from the dueling channels on cable television, there's limited value in a medium that fosters entrenched positions. Collective intelligence is possible only when there is a forum for discovering the common ground among differing points of view.

The second Wikipedia rule is that all content on Wikipedia has to be referenced to a published reliable source. Participants are required to list citations in their articles so that readers can independently verify the information.

This leads to the third rule: Wikipedia does not publish original research. This policy preserves Wikipedia's core mission as an encyclopedia. Professional journals are the place for original research.

The last rule is that participants should assume good faith when working with other Wikipedians. Despite a few rare but well-publicized instances of vandalism on the site, this rule has worked exceedingly well. That's because the extensive ability to verify information in highly transparent environments naturally engenders trust.

Using simple rules to guide complicated efforts is counterintuitive to traditional managers who firmly believe that the key to managing the delivery of a complex set of activities is to monitor all the details. This thinking has reinforced the prevailing expectation in traditional organizations that it's the manager's responsibility to "be on top of everything." As a consequence, staffs spend a large portion of their efforts in time-consuming rituals of control, preparing voluminous reports so that their managers can have access to every project detail. Unfortunately, too many of these reports are left unread because managers simply don't have the time to pore over all the details. This behavior is problematic because, in their zeal to be on top of things, micromanaging bosses wind up slowing things down while the pace of change around them continues to accelerate. Perhaps this explains why so many companies are changing more slowly than the world around them.

While it may seem counterintuitive, it's just as true for humans as it is for colonies of ants or flocks of birds: Simple rules can guide complex collective behavior. Wikipedia—as well as Linux, Gore & Associates, and Morning Star—provides compelling evidence that when large organizations identify a focused set of simple rules that drive effective collective behavior, they need neither bosses nor experts to guide the work. Whether it's the basic protocols employed by Linux and Wikipedia or the clear peer accountability structures used by Gore (see Practice #50) and Morning Star (see Practice #30), the use of simple rules to guide self-directed teams is a far more effective strategy for managing at the pace of change than relying on the continual oversight of a cadre of micromanagers. When leaders have the ability to build a common focus around the few drivers of success, they enable self-organized networks of highly skilled professionals to continually achieve extraordinary performance in an ever-changing world.

PRACTICE #34: NO MORE THAN FOUR. Identifying the critical few performance drivers is not only a highly effective measurement practice; it's also a powerful management discipline that can be extended beyond metrics. What makes this practice so powerful is that it provides a valuable asset that is missing from many organizations: focus. Unless there is a clear sense of focus, it's very difficult for people to connect with the common purpose of their work. Without a shared understanding, people inevitably pursue too many unrelated initiatives, work becomes haphazard and disjointed, and effective execution is hampered by a continual stream of problems and crises. This was the condition of Apple when Steve Jobs returned as CEO in 1997.

One of the reasons for Apple's remarkable turnaround under Jobs's second stint with the technology company was his ability to focus. Upon his return, Jobs conducted a product review that revealed how unfocused Apple had become. Apple was a quagmire of bureaucracy, where unconnected fiefdoms were turning out multiple versions of each product. For example, Apple made a dozen versions of the Macintosh with confusing product numbers ranging from 1400 to 9600.[2] When Jobs asked why Apple was making so many product variations, he learned that his predecessor, Gil Amelio, was convinced that the cure for Apple's deteriorating market position was to make more products. Jobs's response was an immediate 180-degree turn. His strategy was fewer and not more products.

After sitting through the parade of products, Jobs concluded the review by drawing a four-boxed chart on a whiteboard. He labeled the two columns "Consumer" and "Pro" and the two rows "Desktop" and "Portable," and he told his leadership team that their job was to make four great products, one for each quadrant.[3] By focusing on just four areas, Jobs gave Apple's managers and engineers the clarity they needed to build the reputation for product excellence that would become the company's calling card.

Another example of how focusing on no more than four areas produced a great turnaround is the recent renaissance of the Ford Motor Company under Alan Mulally. In the summer of 2006, the carmaker was in the midst of a steady decline. Over the previous five years, its stock price had plummeted by more than half from more than $16 a share to less than $7, and Ford had been surpassed by Toyota, falling from second to third place in worldwide car sales.[4] To solve its problems, Ford's board of directors made what many auto insiders considered a bold move when they reached outside their industry and convinced Mulally to leave Boeing to become the carmaker's new CEO. As the leader of Boeing's Commercial Airplanes Group, Mulally had successfully taken on the formidable challenge from Europe's Airbus Industrie by transforming the company into a lean and profitable enterprise. Ford's board hoped Mulally would do the same for their ailing company.

Upon assuming the leadership of Ford, Mulally brought a sense of focus that had been missing from the dysfunctional management team he inherited. He summarized his plan to return Ford to greatness in four simple points:

1. Aggressively restructure to operate profitably at the current demand and changing model mix.
2. Accelerate development of new products that Ford customers want and value.
3. Finance the plan and improve the balance sheet.
4. Work together effectively as one team.[5]

These four guideposts were reinforced by Mulally in every meeting and interaction he had both inside and outside the company. Ford's focus on these four simple points was largely responsible for putting the company back on the road to profitability.

Although our examples for this practice have been two notable CEOs, No More than Four is a practice that can be used by any manager at any level within almost any organization. By bringing teams together and agreeing on the four most important strategic or tactical activities, managers can build a shared understanding about where they can exercise the greatest leverage in achieving their results. In fast-changing times, the leverage that focus provides is an important key to extraordinary performance.

Resetting the Meetings

PRACTICE #35: ROTATING TABLES. Once an organization has established a clear focus on the most important drivers of its performance, it's important to periodically bring everyone together to reflect upon and understand any new information or developments related to these key indicators. Rather than having a series of monotonous presentations to the full group, managers might consider using the practice of Rotating Tables as a better way to connect with and engage the people who are responsible for delivering the results.

Rotating Tables is a series of twenty- to thirty-minute discussions of four or five concurrent topics where the participants select a different topic for each round of the series. All the participants move from table to table for each of the rounds except for the table facilitators. As the subject experts for the topic, the facilitators remain at the same table for all rounds of the series.

The table facilitators are identified well in advance of the meeting so that they come to the session fully prepared to lead a twenty- to thirty-minute discussion of their topics. Usually, there is one table facilitator per table, although it is acceptable to have two.

So, if there were four topics for the Rotating Tables series, the meeting organizer would write the four topics on a flip chart and assign each of the topics to a particular table. Before beginning the series of discussions, the meeting organizer would inform the participants that:

- They are free to select any table in any order.
- For the first three rounds, they are to select a new topic.
- For the final round, they may select either the final topic or they may repeat a previously selected topic.

At the end of each round, the meeting organizer signals the participants to move to the next table discussion until all the rounds are completed. At the conclusion of the four rounds, the meeting organizer asks each of the table facilitators to summarize the two or three key points that occurred across the discussions that might be of interest to the whole group. The organizer concludes the activity by inviting the participants to share any other key observations from the small group discussions that might be valuable for the whole team.

Processing updates and developments in small groups engages the participants more thoroughly than large group theater-style presentations. That's because more people are likely to join the discussions in small groups, and the discussions will have more of a flow than is possible in a large group question-and-answer session. Greater participation and more effective dialogue enable a deeper understanding of the important information that is critical to driving excellent performance.

PRACTICE #36: DAILY STAND-UP MEETINGS. This is a very widely used practice in Agile software development. Sanjiv Augustine, the author of *Managing Agile Projects*, considers Daily Stand-Up Meetings to be the single most powerful information flow tool in the Agile tool kit.[6] The purpose of this practice is to quickly share key information about the critical activities that drive performance. The daily stand-ups are designed to keep project execution on track and are not useful vehicles for strategic brainstorming or other types of in-depth discussions. Other practices, such as Deep Dives (described below), are designed for more thorough discussions.

What makes Daily Stand-Up Meetings so powerful is that they are brief and focused. These sessions generally last for only fifteen minutes. To facilitate their brevity, all participants meet in a room with no chairs and stand in a circle. Each member is given one or two minutes to update the group on three things:

1. What she worked on yesterday
2. What she plans to work on today
3. What is in her way[7]

These daily sessions make sure that everyone on the team is aware of whether or not the total project is on track, what specific actions are needed to keep the project moving, and how each of the members of the team can support each other to close any gaps as they happen in real time. Because the members meet every day, any tactical issues that may arise are identified and handled immediately and are not given the opportunity to fester into larger problems.

PRACTICE #37: DEEP DIVES. While Daily Stand-Up Meetings are useful tools for making sure that teams execute well by doing things right, Deep Dives are designed to make sure that organizations are strategically focused on doing the right things. Doing things right and doing the right things is not an either/or choice—it's a both/and requirement. The most successful managers excel at both strategy and execution because they understand that one of the fastest ways to business oblivion is to do the wrong things right.

Deep Dives are periodic all-day sessions where leadership teams engage in thoughtful dialogues about the most important issues affecting their business. Depending upon the needs of the team, these sessions are held monthly, biweekly, or weekly, but never less than monthly. This practice can be used by leaders responsible for core business processes, special projects, or key initiatives. Deep Dives is an especially valuable tool for senior leadership teams because it helps them maintain focus in a fast-changing world.

This practice is one of the most difficult for business leaders to adopt because it seems completely counterintuitive. With so many urgent problems and crises bombarding the business, most managers feel that there simply isn't time for engaging in all-day group dialogues. While they would like to devote more time to thinking about the business and would certainly do so if they felt they had a choice, as a practical matter, most managers feel they have more important things that have to be done. When managers are in this frame of mind, they are confusing what's most urgent with what's most important, and they are likely caught up in what the consultants at FranklinCovey call the *whirlwind*.[8]

The whirlwind, according to FranklinCovey, is the energy required to keep the operation going on a day-to-day basis. Because operations are the primary source of a business's most pressing problems, the more urgent issues there are, the greater the intensity of the whirlwind. A highly intense whirlwind is the enemy of innovation because it makes it hard to execute anything new and robs business leaders of the focus they need to move the business forward.[9] Borders, Circuit City, Fannie Mae, Block-buster, and Tower Records are examples of companies that were overtaken by the whirlwind. When the whirlwind overtakes business leaders, they're like lifeguards who get caught in the ferocious grip of a panicked drowning victim. Unless they're willing to do something that feels counterintuitive, they are likely to perish.

There are few things more urgent than saving a swimmer in serious trouble. There's not much time to act because death by drowning is fast and final. In their training, lifeguards are taught a key principle that is counterintuitive to the average swimmer: If a lifeguard ever gets caught in the firm grip of a panicked swimmer, the most important move is to go down under the water. Double drownings happen when would-be rescuers tackled by distressed swimmers expend all their energy in an urgent effort to keep their heads above water. Because a panicked swimmer's instinct is to do everything possible to keep from going under, it's more effective for rescuers to use simple judo techniques to break free from the distressed swimmer's grip, go down and swim away under the water, and resurface several feet away to create a safe space to regroup for a successful rescue. While getting air is urgent for the rescuer, getting free from the grip of the troubled swimmer is what's most important, and by putting the most important need first, the lifeguard is able to safely catch her breath, regroup, and complete the rescue.

As managers struggle to keep up with the relentless pace of change in the wiki world, they need to make sure they don't get caught in the grip of the whirlwind. By periodically regrouping and taking the time to focus on what's most important, they, like well-trained lifeguards, will work smarter rather than harder in meeting all their needs.

Deep Dives was a practice we embraced at the Blue Cross Blue Shield Federal Employee Program (FEP). Once every two weeks, our senior leadership team would meet off-site so we could physically get away from the whirlwind and focus on our most important strategic issues.

Each session began by setting the agenda for the day. While a tentative list of topics was usually distributed a day or two before the session, the final agenda was always established in the first twenty minutes of the meeting. Our first order of business was to confirm our continuing top four strategic priorities, which were usually the first four items on our tentative agenda. Most times, the priorities were confirmed. However, occasionally one of the team members would propose a new priority for the group's consideration. In that instance, we knew that before the session was over, we would need to decide whether or not to include the new issue on our top four priorities list. If we decided to add the topic, it meant we needed to remove another item from the list to be consistent with Practice #34, No More than Four. Our commitment to designate only four strategic issues was the most difficult and the most important part of our team discipline because we forced ourselves to make the choices necessary to be a focused organization.

As team members continued to propose the potential agenda for the day, the team's leader would record the items on a flip chart, including the topic's sponsor and the estimated time needed to thoroughly discuss the item. When the list was complete, the group would quickly by consensus designate the topics, including the original four, as either "A" or "B" items. A items were those that needed to be discussed that day; B items could wait for the next session, if necessary. Each of the A items were then assigned a specific time slot. Any remaining time was assigned to selected items from the B list.

The team leader's primary role in these all-day meetings was to manage our time to make sure that all the A items were understood thoroughly and handled sufficiently. The content of each topic was facilitated by the sponsor who proposed or was primarily responsible for the issue. This practice ensured that leadership for the content of our discussions was distributed across the team. In addition to managing time, another important role for the team's leader was to recognize when the group was stuck and to shift the dynamic of the discussion to move the group along. So, for example, the leader might split the team into two groups and ask members to focus on innovative ways to meet apparently contradictory needs. Another way the leader might move the group along was to ask to hear from one person at a time, with no questions, comments, or interruption until everyone had a chance to speak. Shifting the dynamics of the discussion usually deepened the understanding of the team and allowed us to move forward to higher-level consensus.

These sessions were the lever that enabled us to become a high-performing team. We clearly recognized this when at one point we concluded that the sessions had served their usefulness and weren't necessary anymore, because we appeared to have all our issues under control. We all agreed that we could really use the time that would be freed up by not continuing the sessions. However, after only a few weeks, the team members lobbied to restore the meetings because our effectiveness as a team was slipping as we became distracted by the never-ending parade of the urgent demands of our business. As one team member put it, "While we can't afford the time to have these meetings, what we can't afford even more is not devoting the time to have these sessions."

The primary value of Deep Dives is to make sure that leadership teams have a thorough and shared understanding of the most important strategic issues affecting the project or the business. By deeply understanding what's most important, leadership teams almost always make better decisions when responding to what's most urgent because their direction will reflect proactive rather than reactive thinking. Reactive thinking shuts down options in the face of a crisis, whereas proactive thinking recognizes new opportunities in changing circumstances.

An example of an industry that reinvented itself through proactive thinking is the passenger-ship industry. Before the advent of commercial airlines, the industry was in the oceanic transportation business. As air travel matured and disrupted their business model, the shipping managers realized there was no way they could compete with planes for transoceanic travel. So, they dramatically innovated their business model, entered the vacation business, and remerged far stronger as the cruise industry. It's probably a safe bet that there were some highly effective Deep Dive sessions that preceded that extraordinary transformation.

Resetting the Measures

PRACTICE #38: TOP FOUR PERFORMANCE DRIVERS. This practice is a further refinement of the Balanced Scorecard, the subject of Practice #9. As you will recall, the Balanced Scorecard is an integrated, one-page picture of the business expressed in twelve to twenty key driver and outcome measures across four balanced perspectives. Once the measures in the scorecard are agreed upon, it is often useful for management teams to revisit the driver measures and identify the four most important measures among them. These four measures can provide a powerful frame of reference as a communication tool for aligning the distributed work throughout the organization with what's most important to the company's success.

The metrics for the top four performance drivers should be widely broadcast throughout the organization because the knowledge of how the organization is doing on its critical few measures can serve the same purpose in organizations as the simple set of rules that guides the journey of a flock of birds. If it is true that what gets measured gets managed, then a well-communicated focus of the critical few performance drivers ensures that all the workers in the company are doing their part to influence key business outcomes by making the connections between their jobs and the key drivers of success.

At Blue Cross Blue Shield FEP, we posted the status of our four most important performance drivers on the walls of every floor of our offices. The daily reinforcement of our progress on our key leading indicators was a major contributing factor to the positive turnaround in our growth and performance.

PRACTICE #39: THE ONE NUMBER. Do you know the most important number for your business? Do you know the one number that will tell you whether you are highly likely to meet or miss your key performance goals? Is it your company's stock price or perhaps its earnings per share? Is it the most recent year's revenues or market share? While all of these numbers are important, none of them are candidates for the one most important number for your business. Hopefully, you recognized that each one of the numbers proposed was an outcome measure, and as we learned before, while performance metrics are ultimately important because they let us know whether or not we met our business targets, they are nevertheless poor management tools because, once the results are in, there's nothing we can do to influence or change them. Therefore, the One Number is never a lagging indicator—it is always a leading indicator. In fact, it is the most important leading indicator of the business.

In his well-known study of good-to-great companies, Jim Collins found that one of the distinguishing characteristics of the exceptional organizations is that every one of them had attained a deep understanding of the key driver of their economic engine in the form of a single "economic denominator."[10] This number is usually a ratio, in which the significance may not be immediately self-evident. Collins cites the example of Walgreen's, which, in discovering its One Number, shifted its focus from profit per store to profit per customer visit.[11] While store profitability is the ultimate financial goal, tracking this number doesn't provide any insight into what matters most to customers. When Walgreen's executives switched their focus to profit per customer visit, they tapped into real-time information that put them in touch with why customers visited their stores. By understanding what mattered most to the customers, Walgreen's was better poised to meet their needs, which was reflected in the favorable metrics of the ratio of profit per customer visit. In discovering their One Number, Walgreen's managers gave themselves a powerful tool for driving increased store profitability.

We made a similar discovery at Blue Cross Blue Shield FEP. The key financial metric in the health insurance business is number of months of reserves. As a rule, health insurance managers are comfortable when they have two to three months of reserves. These reserves are important because they provide a cushion that allows an insurance company to handle unexpected events, such as an epidemic or a dramatic change in the demographic mix of its covered population. This cushion also provides insurers with the ability to maintain stable premium rates because they don't have an urgent need to immediately restore their lost funds to remain solvent when the unexpected occurs.

However, number of months of reserves is an outcome measure, and we wanted to be proactive in maintaining a stable cushion in our reserves. This had been notably challenging for us in the early 1980s, when we had dropped to a single day's worth of claims payments, and it then took the remainder of the decade to restore our reserves to acceptable levels. The particular population we covered required skillful management because we had an equal mix of active workers and retirees. With such a high number of retirees (who generally use more medical services), maintaining a healthy balance of workers and retirees was critical to our preserving the stable rates we needed to remain attractive to younger workers. We knew the retirees would remain with us because Blue Cross Blue Shield was a brand that they had bonded with over many years. Our challenge was to remain attractive to the relatively healthier workers to maintain the needed balance in our demographic mix. That's when we discovered a metric that we had not been previously monitoring: the net active ratio.

The net active ratio is the number of new active worker enrollments as a percent of total new enrollments for the previous month. If the ratio indicated that a high proportion of the new enrollments were active workers, it let us know that we were either maintaining or improving our enrollment mix. A healthy demographic mix meant we were highly likely to preserve our reserves and maintain reasonable premium rates. The stable rates, in turn, allowed us to attract more active workers and helped enable a virtuous cycle.

Discovering our One Number was another important contributing factor to the remarkable growth we experienced at FEP. While the ratio was consistently favorable during my time with FEP, had the number turned negative, we would have been able to both reflect and act on what we needed to do long before the downturn affected our reserves. We would have had time to take either the corrective or adaptive actions needed to avert any negative impact on our reserves. Even in the face of impending change, we would have been able to influence our outcomes. That's the power of knowing your One Number.

CHAPTER SUMMARY: KEY POINTS

→ All measures are not the same. Some measures are more important than others. In fact, in any project or activity, there are usually a handful of measures that are the key indicators of ultimate success or failure.

→ In the identification of the critical few performance drivers, the most important leading indicators are not always intuitively obvious and many times may actually appear to be counterintuitive.

→ A simple yet pervasively misunderstood rule of business is that you can't manage results by tracking results. You can manage results only by tracking the drivers of results.

→ Leading indicators let managers know if their expected results are likely to occur, but more importantly, if it appears that the business is underperforming, they provide managers with sufficient time to make the right decision between two very different courses of actions: Do they correct or do they adapt?

→ If it is true that what gets measured gets managed, a well communicated focus of the critical few performance drivers ensures that all the workers in the company are doing their part to influence key business outcomes by making the connections between their jobs and the key drivers of success.

8

Hold People Accountable
to Their Peers

When your mission is to guard the globe against epidemics, success is not measured in dollars and cents but rather in lives saved and deaths prevented. When your work issues are literally matters of life and death, there's no time for bureaucracy. Disease control scientists know that collaboration is essential when speedy innovation is an imperative for containing a potential global pandemic. In one thirty-day period in the early spring of 2003, the world witnessed the remarkable efficiency of the mass collaboration of society's community of scientists, but because they did their work so well, most of us barely noticed.

In late November 2002, scientists at Canada's Global Public Health Intelligence Network (GPHIN), while routinely monitoring Internet media, observed reports of a possible flu outbreak in China and forwarded this information to the World Health Organization (WHO).[1] In early December, the WHO requested a report from Chinese authorities. The WHO was assured by the government that its investigation into the appearance of the virus indicated that the number of cases identified was completely consistent with the seasonal patterns observed in previous years.[2] However, in February 2003, the Chinese Ministry of Health reversed itself and reported to the WHO that 305 people had been stricken with a severe respiratory disease, and five of them had died.[3] Over the next several weeks, the WHO tested several virus specimens in its laboratories and was able to conclusively rule out the influenza virus as the cause of the illness. By mid-March, WHO authorities were certain that they were dealing with an entirely new disease, which they named SARS (for severe acute respiratory syndrome), and they also knew that they needed to isolate the root cause to avoid a potential pandemic.

On March 17, 2003, the WHO initiated a global effort involving eleven research laboratories from countries around the world, which was called a "collaborative multicenter research project."[4] If the WHO was to prevent a pandemic, it was a given that the agency had to organize its efforts to leverage the collective intelligence of the world's best epidemiologists. In daily conference calls, scientists around the globe shared their observations and analyses, debated the results, and explored future avenues for their research. Through these daily calls, using the data that they were continually passing back and forth among all the laboratories, they were able to learn quickly from each other and aggregate their dispersed observations into a developing collective knowledge.

Within a matter of days, scientists at both Hong Kong University and the Centers for Disease Control and Prevention in the United States had separately identified the possible culprit of the new disease, and—after further research in labs in Germany, the Netherlands, and Hong Kong— the scientists were certain that the identified coronavirus was indeed the cause of SARS.[5] After a mere thirty days from the start of the scientific collaboration, on April 16, 2003, the WHO was able to announce its crucial discovery to the world. The agency was then able to provide specific guidance for clinical treatment to health professionals and was also able to make recommendations to international travelers to prevent the spread of the disease.[6] The quick work of this collaborative community was so successful that, on July 5, 2003, the WHO confidently declared that the SARS outbreak had been contained.

We are fortunate that the WHO did not have direct authority over the international community of scientists. Otherwise, we might have seen a research command center rather than a collaborative multicenter research project. If the SARS research effort had been organized into a centralized bureaucratic structure, it most likely would have taken months instead of weeks to find the root cause of the new disease. Politics invariably finds its way into centralized structures and distracts an organization from its core purpose by slowing down the pursuit of truth to manage perceptions. Centralized bureaucracies sometimes put their interests in looking good ahead of getting it right. That is exactly what happened when the Chinese government encountered the early cases of SARS. The government at first downplayed the seriousness of the public health threat and characterized the early instances as nothing more than the flu. The government finally came forward with the complete facts only after chatter on the Internet made spinning the story impossible. While the government was focused on managing perceptions, precious time was wasted—time that could have been better used pursuing the analysis of the cause of the new disease.

The SARS experience demonstrates how highly effective peer-to-peer communities can be when they have a clear and compelling mission. No centralized organization, or even a single individual, could have discovered the cause of SARS in only thirty days. Only a mass collaboration of self-organizing professionals can uncover the unknown with that kind of speed. In the SARS story, as typically happens in successful mass collaborative ventures, there were no individual heroes or self-promoting bosses taking the limelight. Perhaps that's why most of us barely remember the episode. Despite the absence of obvious heroes, solving SARS was truly a heroic effort—only this time the hero was a global team. Every one of the scientists in the collaboration is responsible for finding the cause of SARS. And the scientists are perfectly fine with that because they fully appreciate what most businesses will soon learn if they hope to succeed in the wiki world: A self-organizing team of collegial peers collaborating in a horizontal network usually works smarter and faster than traditional hierarchies and individual heroes.

OPEN SOURCE COMMUNITIES

The Digital Revolution and its technological innovations are creating entirely new ways of working together that only twenty years ago would have stretched the limits of believability. Who would have imagined that you could build a successful computer operating system by assembling a community of unsupervised volunteers, and that the product these freelancers put together would be so good that the historical leader of the information technology industry would abandon its own proprietary offerings to become part of the online community? Yet that is the incredible story of Linux and the emerging power of peer-based open source technology.

In 1991, Linus Torvalds, a graduate student at the University of Helsinki, came up with an innovative idea for creating a new computer operating system. Relying on the efforts of volunteer programmers around the world, Torvalds used the long established Unix language as a model for a state-of-the-art system that he dubbed Linux. Because Torvalds knew that computer programmers are a unique breed of people who love to interact and impress each other with their knowledge, he posted his initial source code for Linux on an online bulletin board and invited other programmers to build upon his work. A handful of programmers responded almost immediately with substantial changes, and it wasn't long before others joined the effort, spawning over time a virtual collaborative community of software engineers bonded by their pride as innovators in the creation of a truly first-class product. As interest in the software continued to grow, Torvalds decided to make the operating system commercially available under a general public license so that anyone could use it for free as long as each user agreed that any changes made to the program remain in the public domain and available to everyone.[7]

The growing popularity of this innovative approach to software development caught the attention of one traditional computer corporation, which recognized that it might be time to make a radical change from its old ways of thinking. IBM had been playing catch-up in the PC market by attempting, with much cost and little success, to build its own proprietary operating system to compete with Microsoft's dominant Windows application. However, despite IBM's best efforts, the brutal market reality was becoming quite clear to the company's executives: Big Blue was too late to the market to expect success in building its own commercial product, and sinking more money into this initiative was a guaranteed loser. Nevertheless, it was also clear that IBM's competitiveness in the computer services and solutions market was dependent upon its ability to provide affordable operating systems for those customers seeking alternatives. To solve its dilemma, IBM recognized that it would need to abandon its longstanding notions of proprietary ownership, take an unorthodox leap into the public domain of open source technology, and completely transform the way its programmers worked. IBM made a bold strategic move and joined the Linux community of volunteer programmers.

IBM's alliance with Linux is a win-win for both organizations. With the addition of a multitude of IBM software experts, Linux's programming efforts receive a boost valued at $100 million per year.[8] For its part, at only 20 percent of the cost of a proprietary offering, Big Blue is able to develop and distribute an operating system that is compatible with its other product lines at no additional charge to its customers.[9] But perhaps the greatest value for IBM from its venture into the world of open source technology is its discovery of the power of peer-to-peer collaborations. Because of its Linux experience, IBM has firsthand knowledge of how today's challenge of organizing the work of large numbers of people is less about bosses and work assignments and more about leveraging the self-organized efforts of an effective community of peers.

PEERS OVER SUPERVISORS

The SARS experience and the emergence of open source communities are two examples of the innovative architecture of a radically different organizational structure that is dramatically redefining the practice of management. In a post-digital world, the power that comes from being connected trumps the power of being in charge. The vanguard companies that fully appreciate this principle include many of the companies whose practices are highlighted in this book: Google, W.L. Gore & Associates, Morning Star, Valve, Whole Foods, Wikipedia, and Zappos. Each of these organizations has been consciously designed to maximize human interaction, encourage employee engagement, enable the dynamics of serendipity and emergence, and foster a culture of innovation. At the heart of this conscious design is a deliberate effort to eliminate the traditional sovereignty of the supervisor, and, in some instances, to do away with supervisors altogether. Every one of these companies understands that in fast-changing times, managing innovation works best when people are accountable to peers rather than supervisors.

The single greatest obstacle to innovation is the chain of command that defines the hierarchical organization. That's because, in traditional companies, too many people have the authority to kill good ideas or keep bad ideas alive. This was the primary insight and the fundamental organizing principle for Bill Gore, as we learned in Chapter 2, when he eschewed the traditional supervisor–subordinate relationship and built his lattice organization. Organizations that are built for innovation cannot afford the hindrances of the egos of a cadre of supervisors. If they are to keep pace with the speed of change, they cannot allow a good idea to be stopped by a single boss, or the value of a suggestion to be weighted by the position of the speaker, nor can they tolerate a glacial bureaucracy that fails to meet evolving customer expectations or is too slow to recognize that customer values have shifted. That's why it is so important to eliminate the sovereignty of the supervisors.

The basis for managerial power no longer comes from dominating the thinking or directing the work of others; rather, it now comes from integrating the best of everyone's ideas and building highly effective collaborative networks. In contrast to traditional hierarchies, which limit the interpersonal influence of the many through the ascription of authority, the power structures of wiki-world companies amplify the opportunities for the development of relationships across all the people within an organizational network. The more connections there are, the greater the opportunities for collaboration and innovation, which are the prime drivers for sustained success in fast-changing markets.

Each of the vanguard companies is designed to enable collaboration and innovation. Accordingly, each has embraced an organizational architecture where the workers are responsible for results, where colleagues are expected to collaborate with each other, and where everyone is clear that he works for the customer. In these leading-edge businesses, people are accountable to many colleagues rather than to a single supervisor.

When workers are accountable for results and to each other and are able to act on their own shared understanding, there's no finger-pointing or playing the blame game that's so typical in hierarchical bureaucracies. If people are accountable only for their individual tasks and to single supervisors, they can sit back and watch processes fall apart as long as their tasks are complete. However, when people are accountable for results and to each other, they all fail when a business process breaks down, and after-the-fact finger-pointing becomes meaningless. In the wiki world, self-organized work is more effective than assignments by supervisors because knowledge workers are far more motivated by their standing with their professional peers than they are by pleasing the bosses. As a result, they are more willing to assume responsibility to make sure everything works.

The most difficult adjustment for managers as they embrace the five disciplines of Wiki Management is coming to terms with their new role as the facilitators and catalysts of effective peer-to-peer collaboration. However, the vanguard companies are compelling examples of how organizations can become incredibly effective when the sovereignty of the supervisor is diminished.

TRANSPARENCY OVER CONTROL

A concern that many managers may have as they consider transitioning worker accountability from supervisors to peers is how they will be able to maintain the control they feel is necessary for the business to succeed. If people are primarily accountable to peers, are they not setting themselves up for complete chaos?

While it may appear counterintuitive, an important lesson we learn from the complexity sciences is that giving up control and embracing a little chaos at the beginning of projects often leads to a more effective state of control in the end. By building a shared understanding and then delegating the exercise of control to the workers who actually do the work, companies are not only more responsive to changing circumstances, but are actually more controlled at the same time. The degree of transparency needed to build an effective shared understanding provides collaborative organizations with a higher-order control system than is ever possible in bureaucratic hierarchies.

Transparency is the most effective control system because when everyone knows everything, there are no secrets. Companies with high levels of freedom of information and freedom of action have more resources available to them to ensure that the business remains under control. As a result, problems don't fester, innovation is not muted, and quality is continually improved. This explains why W.L. Gore & Associates, which has never had supervisors in its fifty-plus years, is so much better controlled than many of its command-and-control counterparts. The level of transparency needed to make Gore's consensus management work eliminates the hidden agendas and the institutional ignorance that plague organizations when secrets prevail. While Gore's processes are more chaotic at the start of projects, the thorough understanding needed to move a team of peers forward leads to greater employee engagement and more reliable results at the end of the work.

Traditional organizations have lots of secrets. With work subdivided among departments and directed by managers who are often engaged in some form of "turf battle," it's not surprising that information does not flow freely and that many workers are unaware of what people do outside their own departments. Sometimes the secrets are intentional, such as when information is shared on a "need-to-know" basis or even deliberately withheld. More often than not, most corporate secrets are the unintentional consequences of the functional fragmentation of work. Whatever the reason, hierarchical organizations breed secrets. And that explains why they need elaborate control systems.

When secrets prevail, there is little or no shared understanding among either the managers or the workers to guide consistent delivery of customer value. Worse yet, without the transparency that naturally accompanies shared understanding, there could be plenty of opportunities for greedy or malicious employees to defraud the company. To protect themselves from the potential adverse consequences of bureaucratic secrets, hierarchical organizations promulgate a constant stream of rules and regulations and establish complex control structures based on checks and balances. These structures rely upon armies of supervisors and auditors to ensure that everyone is following the rules and that people are not using their secrets to inappropriately enrich themselves. The theory is that if everyone has someone watching over him, the risks associated with the inevitable secrets in bureaucracies will be mitigated and the business will be under control. The unfortunate irony, however, is that often the application of complex rules and regulations only slows things down, creates confusion, and actually weakens control.

The only way that managers, coping with the challenges of accelerating changes, can remain consistently in control is by moving away from centralized authority to decentralized transparency. This means that pertinent business knowledge needs to be freely shared among all the workers and that all related data and metrics have to be continually available to everyone. It also means that the individual workers need to be available to each other. Transparency isn't just about everybody knowing everything. It also means that everybody is available to everyone. Without both of these dimensions, true transparency is not possible.

When companies have the benefit of high-order transparency, managers don't have to depend upon the representations of other managers or auditors to ensure that the business is running smoothly. They can take comfort in the fact that when all workers have access to everything, if there's something they need to know, they'll find out sooner rather than later because when everyone is available to everybody, there are no secrets.

PRACTICES

The following are actual practices used by companies to hold people accountable to their peers. Given your role within your organization and the current state of your corporate culture, some practices may work better than others. Focus on two or three practices that would best work in your particular business circumstances.

Resetting the Managers

PRACTICE #40: KILL THE KILLER. The single greatest threat to the survival of many companies could very well come from their own managers. That certainly was on Bill Gore's mind when he founded W.L. Gore & Associates in 1958. In Chapter 2, we learned how Gore created a radically different approach to organizing the work of large numbers of people. In designing what he called a lattice organization, his guiding principle was that no one, not even Gore himself, should have the authority to kill a good idea or keep a bad idea alive. Gore understood that innovative ideas usually challenge the status quo and often require organizations to venture into unfamiliar territory. Despite all the rhetoric about embracing change and venturing into new horizons, Gore knew that the vast majority of managers prefer the status quo and are very hesitant to disrupt the positional authority they hold in their existing operational models. That's why traditional managers much prefer incremental to disruptive change.

However, Gore was not a traditional manager, and he wanted to create a company that was designed to promote and enable disruptive innovation. To do that, he needed to kill the role that allows people to kill good ideas. He needed to kill the killer, and the only way that he could do that was to make sure that there were no bosses. Whether ideas lived or died would not be subject to the whims of a single supervisor; instead, the collective wisdom of accountable peers would ultimately decide what work the company did or didn't do.

W.L. Gore & Associates is not alone in embracing the practice of Kill the Killer. Morning Star, the Northern California tomato processor, and Valve, the Bellevue, Washington, video gaming company—we met both in Chapter 6—also have no supervisors and have successfully mastered the practice of bosslessness. While it may be difficult, even inconceivable, for traditional managers to comprehend, the sustained market success of Gore, Morning Star, and Valve are compelling evidence that it is possible to manage highly effective organizations without bosses.

However, managers who might contemplate emulating Gore's lattice organization need to follow two critical prerequisites to realize the full power of self-organization. The first is that all the different contributors on a project need to be together in the same place (see Practice #24). This means that product design, sales, marketing, and production staffs work together in cross-functional teams so that everyone continually understands how their contributions shape and reshape the underlying business processes of the company's value proposition. Bill Gore recognized the value of having everyone in the same room at the same time and the importance of having workers focused on collective processes rather than individual tasks.

Second, Gore noticed that things got awkward when the number of workers reached about 150 to 200 people. There seems to be a tipping point in the human scale where the effectiveness of peer pressure and the physical ability to self-organize begins to break down.[10] When there are more than 200 people in the same location, the individuals don't feel as personally connected to each other and it becomes difficult even to know everyone's name. We can understand why, in the early factories of the Industrial Age, the owners resorted to hierarchical management to organize the work of large numbers of people. When the efforts of a sizable group of workers have to be brought together and there are so many people that they can't possibly all know each other, the corporate pioneers of mass production felt that authoritative bosses were necessary to get the job done. Bill Gore, however, did not want to resort to the employment of bosses when he noticed the tipping point. Instead, he put in place a simple practice to preserve his self-organizing management innovation that continues to this day. When a plant approaches 200 people, the group divides, and Gore opens another plant. The new plant may be a stone's throw from the original location, but each plant is completely autonomous to ensure the human scale necessary for self-organization to work.

When employing the practice of Kill the Killer, it's very important to make sure that you don't inadvertently kill the work. These two important prerequisites should not be overlooked because they can mean the difference between aimless chaos or extraordinary performance when companies decide to go bossless.

PRACTICE #41: THE 60:1 RULE. Designing a company without supervisors is not an option for most existing companies and usually works best when the lattice structure is built into the original design of the organization. Nevertheless, the problem of too many people having the authority to kill good ideas needs to be effectively handled if existing organizations want to sustain themselves in an increasingly innovative world. While business leaders may not be able to eliminate the supervisors, a commitment to innovation means they at least need to eliminate the sovereignty of their supervisors.

One of the most effective ways to eliminate supervisory sovereignty is to adopt a practice developed by Sergey Brin and Larry Page at Google when it grew to a point where it was no longer an intimate company where everyone knew each other.

When Google passed the tipping point of 150 people around the start of the new millennium, a layer of middle management began emerging in the growing organization as many of the new hires came from more traditionally structured companies.[11] When the company reached 400 people in 2001, Brin and Page became concerned that a steadily creeping bureaucracy would inevitably destroy the bottom-up style of management they cherished. Their response was to eliminate all the managers. However, somewhat to the founders' surprise, bosslessness wasn't well received by the Google staffers. When Page asked why, the staff members replied that they wanted someone they could learn from and who could referee disagreements when colleagues had reached an impasse.[12]

Realizing that they had to accommodate the needs of the staffers, Brin and Page devised an innovative win-win solution. If they couldn't eliminate the supervisors, they could at least diminish the influence of the supervisors. Their solution was to install the 60:1 Rule, which still works today. The typical supervisor at Google has approximately sixty direct reports. This ratio ensures that staffers have managers who can serve as both mentors and referees, while making it virtually impossible for those supervisors to micromanage their staffs because it's humanly impossible to closely monitor sixty people.

PRACTICE #42: THE 20% RULE. This is another practice that Google uses to eliminate the sovereignty of the supervisor. While most companies proclaim a commitment to innovation, few managers actually devote meaningful resources to weave innovation into the fabric of their management system. Innovation isn't a functional task that can be delegated to a department or a special assignment team; it's a different way of working that involves everyone in an organization. The leaders at Google understand what a commitment to innovation means, which is why they are ardent practitioners of the 20% Rule.

Most of the employees at Google are allowed to devote 20 percent of their time to work on projects of their choosing. The workers are free to follow their passions without regard for their managers' opinions of the worthiness of their pet projects. Sergey Brin and Larry Page borrowed the practice from 3M, whose highly profitable innovation, Post-it Notes, might never have happened without the 20% Rule. 3M's executives had initially dismissed the idea for Post-It Notes. However, two 3M scientists used their "20 percent" time to follow their intuitions and successfully demonstrate the market value for what would become one of the company's most lucrative product lines.

Brin and Page were drawn to the practice because it wove an important dynamic from their graduate school days into Google's management system.[13] Graduate students at Standford, in addition to their regular studies, are encouraged by their professors to pursue self-selected projects. This pursuit of their own passions is what led Brin and Page to create their innovative search engine. They wanted this same dynamic to be the lifeblood of their management model. In designing their organization, Brin and Page understood a powerful management lesson that eludes most traditional managers: Innovation happens in the intersection of time and passion. Unfortunately, most employees in traditionally managed companies suffer from severe shortages in both of these key ingredients.

Marissa Mayer, the former Google executive who is now the CEO of Yahoo, credits the 20% Rule for delivering half of Google's new products.[14] The practice encourages employees to push the envelope and to disrupt the traditional ways of doing things. Allowing workers to self-direct a significant chunk of their time to follow their passions is one of the ways Google sustains its innovative edge.

PRACTICE #43: ACCOUNTABILITY PARTNERS. This is a simple and powerful practice that can be used, either formally or informally, in any organization. All it requires is two people who are willing to support each other in achieving results. The practice of Accountability Partners is a co-mentoring process in which two people meet periodically, usually every four to six weeks, for a two-hour, one-on-one session. In these sessions, they take turns reviewing each other's progress on achieving key business and professional goals. For the first hour, one person reports on progress made since the previous session while the other serves as a coach, providing encouragement and assistance to his partner. During the second hour, they reverse roles and discuss the progress of the second person.

These sessions are powerful because they provide the opportunity for a cadence of candid accountability that drives both business results and professional growth. This opportunity works best when there is a high level of trust between the two partners, which is why individuals should be free to choose their own partners. In a safe atmosphere of mutual trust, the partners have the space to engage in crucial conversations to discuss what's working and not working, and to provide mutual guidance to drive real and lasting positive change.

Candidates for accountability partnerships can come from almost anywhere in the organization. The only exception is that one's direct supervisor is usually not a good candidate for this role. Supervisors are generally required to make formal judgments about their subordinates' performance that could interfere with the candor that makes accountability partnerships work.

Typically, accountability partners are peers, although there are times when it may be valuable to select a partner from a different organizational level. For example, a senior leader might select a junior person as an accountability partner as a way to better understand the impact of new technologies on the business or the unintended consequences of the executive's decisions. The junior person, in turn, has the opportunity for a powerful mentoring relationship. This pairing of senior and junior partners can work only if the two individuals completely trust each other, which means the senior person must make it safe for the junior person to be completely candid.

Perhaps the most important dynamic of this accountability relationship is that the high level of trust makes it possible for the two people to discuss their blind spots. These blind spots are the things that *everybody knows about you except for you.* In my own personal experience with this practice, especially as a senior leader, learning about my blind spots and having a mentor who could guide me through the changes I needed to make greatly improved my effectiveness as a leader.

PRACTICE #44: TEMPORARY LEADERS. In the hierarchical organization, career growth is about moving up the ladder to higher and higher positions of permanent leadership. Once a person is designated as the head of the department, he is usually in that role until he either moves up to a more senior role or moves out and leaves the organization.

At W.L. Gore & Associates, however, there is no hierarchy and no ladder, and leadership is generally a temporary role. Career growth is a function of one's continuing skills and experience rather than one's title.

At Gore, no leader ever appoints another leader. Instead, leaders are chosen by the members of self-organized work teams based on the needs of the project at the time. As a consequence, leadership is temporary and situational. In the early phases of a project, someone who is skilled in brainstorming and building consensus might emerge as the initial leader to guide the group in formulating its vision and strategy. Once the mission of the project is clear, a member who is an effective project manager might take the lead in constructing and monitoring the building of the group's deliverable. Still another member of the group who has excellent client relationships might be asked by the team to lead the marketing efforts of the new product. And, finally, when the new product is fully operational, the team that built it may disband and another team might assimilate the developed product into its mature-product mix.

As organizational structures shift from hierarchies to networks and transform themselves into highly effective self-organized arrangements, the notion of career ladders and the permanent leadership positions they spawn will become obsolete. In a fast-changing world, business and operating models are continually changing, and very little remains permanent. The self-organized dynamics of networked organizations such as Gore are a window into the future of leadership.

Resetting the Meetings

PRACTICE #45: MILESTONE TIMELINES. This practice is very useful at the start of complex projects when large groups of people who are normally physically or geographically dispersed are brought together to coordinate their efforts. Milestone Timelines are usually the final activity in these collaboration sessions.

The leader prepares the meeting room by taping a row of blank flip chart pages across a large wall space. Each flip chart page represents a month, and the leader writes the name of the month at the top of each page in chronological order (i.e., March, April, May, etc.). The leader then asks the participants to identify key dates for the important milestones that need to be met to successfully deliver the project. The leader instructs the group that the milestones do not have to be identified in chronological order; rather, as individuals think of key tasks, they can record them on the calendar pages.

For example, if the group is working on a nine-month project to install a new customer service center that needs to be operational by the end of October, the first participant might identify the obvious activity of having the customer service center operational on October 31. The leader would then record at the bottom of the October page, "31—Customer Service Center Operational." The next participant might identify the necessary recruitment activities for customer service representatives (CSRs), with job postings starting on June 1 and all staff hired and reporting for work on September 30. The facilitator would record at the top of the June page, "1—Job Postings for CSR Staff," and at the bottom of the September page, "30—All CSRs Hired/Start Work."

As the participants continue to identify activities, misalignments may begin to surface. For example, participants from the business area may be focused on a completion date of September 30 for the CSR manual so that it's ready for the CSR training scheduled for the month of October. The participants responsible for training might point out that a September 30 completion date for the training manual will not work because time will be needed to train the trainers if the October CSR training is to be effective. As a result, the completion date for the training manual might be modified to August 31 to provide sufficient time for training the trainers. The identification and recording of activities and the appropriate adjustments to the original dates of activities continue until all key activities are captured on the flip chart pages and everyone in the room is comfortable with the timeline.

The practice of Milestone Timelines is powerful because the timelines accomplish three things. First, the complete end-to-end process of activities that are critical to success are properly sequenced in time, thus facilitating the effective execution of on-time quality deliverables. Second, by focusing on the project as an integrated process rather than as a distribution of specific tasks, misalignments of tasks are identified before the work begins. How many times in command-and-control organizations do we see tasks for key initiatives distributed among functional departments without people understanding how their jobs interrelate with those of their colleagues in other departments? When this happens, the project is likely to run into difficulties in the later phases as different departments have differing understandings of the timing of activities in the project. Milestone Timelines eliminate eleventh-hour crises by front-ending the misalignments and fully resolving them at the start of the project. This saves companies both time and money.

The third and most powerful contribution of Milestone Timelines is the creation of a shared understanding among all the project participants. Each person has a clear picture of the whole process and fully understands the interrelationships among the activities and how his tasks fit into the overall project. By participating in the construction of the holistic timeline, witnessing the conversations as critical potential misalignments are identified and resolved, and visually seeing the entire project mapped on the calendar flip chart pages, all participants go back to their departments or locations working toward the same timeline. It is far more powerful for people in organizations to be working to timelines where they truly understand how their part fits into the whole project than to be working to due dates assigned by a boss.

When individuals work to shared timelines that they have helped create, they understand why they cannot be late with their tasks and the full ramifications that missed deadlines have on the project. On the other hand, if individuals are working merely to due dates, it's very easy to think that missing a deadline by a few days won't matter much. Yet those few days could mean the difference between the ultimate success and failure of the project.

PRACTICE #46: ON-THE-SPOT AGENDA. On-the-Spot Agenda meetings are especially useful for improving the working relationships between two departments that have a history of hostile turf battles. This meeting format was one we used at the Blue Cross Blue Shield Federal Employee Program with remarkable success, often transforming functional feuds into collaborative partnerships. What's most interesting about this practice is that it breaks the most fundamental rule about how to run an effective meeting.

Conventional wisdom dictates that the best meetings are those where there is a clearly established agenda that is distributed in advance of the meeting. This way, the participants can review pertinent materials beforehand and come to the meetings fully prepared. When the participants are highly effective collaborators, this rule works very well.

But what happens when the participants are caught up in intense turf battles? Quite often, the early distribution of the agenda puts in play a set of dysfunctional dynamics that renders the scheduled meeting useless. First, there are the unofficial "meetings" before the meeting, where differing groups caucus among themselves so they can appear cooperative while guarding their turf, decide what information they will share and withhold, and figure out how to dominate their perceived opponent. While the feuding departments are fully prepared when the actual meeting occurs, little actually gets done because the most important issues are often avoided to limit internal political vulnerability.

The innovative dynamic that makes on-the-spot meetings work is the elimination of the early distribution of the agenda. This, in turn, eliminates the meetings before the meeting and defuses the internal politicking. Instead, the participants of the two departments schedule a meeting for a specific time frame (e.g., two hours) and agree that defining the agenda will be the first order of business when the session begins. The rules for setting the agenda are similar to those used in Deep Dives (Practice #37) and are as follows:

- The leaders of the two departments serve as the meeting facilitators and do *not* propose agenda items.

- Agenda topics and the expected amount of time needed to handle each topic are proposed by the staff members and are recorded on a flip chart by one of the meeting facilitators.

- After all topics are proposed, the participants collectively designate each of the topics as either "A" or "B" items. A items are those that need to be discussed that day; B items can wait for the next time the group gets together, if necessary. Each of the A items is assigned a specific time slot, and any remaining time is assigned to selected items from the B list.

- The discussion of the content of each topic is led by the staff member who proposed the topic. The two department leaders manage the timing of the meeting to make sure that the group adheres to its schedule. While the department managers may participate in the discussions, neither serves as the leader of any of the topical discussions.

By following these simple rules, two groups that have not worked well together begin discussing their most important issues. As they move to effective solutions, hardened barriers often start to break down, and a workable level of cooperation takes hold. When this practice is highly successful, departmental wars are supplanted by genuine collaboration.

Resetting the Measures

PRACTICE #47: TRUE COLORS. Sometimes the most effective measures aren't numbers. There are times when colors are better conveyers of the most important information. When Alan Mulally became the CEO of Ford, one of his first actions was to install the weekly Business Plan Review (BPR) discipline that had worked so well during his time at Boeing. In these sessions, each member of the leadership team presents a concise color-coded update of his progress toward meeting key company goals.

Projects that are on track or ahead of schedule are colored green, yellow indicates the initiative has potential issues or concerns, and red denotes those programs that are behind schedule or off plan.[15]

Color-coded status reports provide a level of transparency that is sometimes absent from the usual numerical reports, and processing these visual updates as a team instills a discipline of peer accountability that is often lacking in leadership teams. The cadence of frequently gathering the whole team in one place to review all key initiatives helps to create a shared understanding about the most important issues of the business. But more important, as happened in the case of Ford, it provides critical opportunities for the team members to synchronize their activities to help create extraordinary performance.

When implementing the practice of True Colors, the leader needs to maintain an environment where it is safe to candidly report the actual status of key activities. There's no value in status meetings where everyone reports that all is well—even when things are not—because people are more concerned with maintaining an image than dealing with reality. When members of a team have a process where it is safe to tell the truth about the actual state of their projects, they provide themselves with the opportunities to assist each other to more quickly resolve critical issues when they occur. The primary purpose of peer accountability is not to create more pressure for individual performance but rather to identify opportunities for the team to leverage its collective strength. The practice of True Colors is a very effective way to provide those opportunities.

PRACTICE #48: AUTONOMOUS PEER INPUT. As a way to promote teamwork, many companies encourage supervisors to canvass people within and outside their departments as they prepare performance reviews for their subordinates. However, this input is usually filtered by supervisors who ultimately decide whether or not to include the observations in the written performance reviews. Thus, if two departments don't get along, a supervisor might easily dismiss the negative observations of peers in the other department, even though customers would be better served if the staff in the two departments found better ways to work together.

A key dimension of holding people accountable to their peers is allowing for direct and unfiltered peer input. The practice of Autonomous Peer Input helps diminish the sovereignty of the supervisor by eliminating the boss's ability to filter or censor the input of key internal partners. As part of the annual review process, the performance evaluation tool is modified to include a section where key peers rate the performance and provide feedback for the employee review. This input cannot be filtered or edited by the employee's supervisor.

The practice of Autonomous Peer Input sends a clear signal across the organization that pleasing the boss is not the only pathway to success in the company. In collaborative networks, people have to build relationships and coordinate effectively with others to meet their common goals. The relationship with a worker's supervisor is just one—and not necessarily the most important—of those relationships. While this practice may appear to place an additional burden on employees who have to learn how to balance the needs of both their supervisors and peers, promoting a culture of peer accountability provides a better foundation for building the level of collaboration companies need to effectively manage in today's hyper-connected wiki world.

PRACTICE #49: UPWARD EVALUATIONS. In organizations that have supervisors, an important aspect of the discipline of peer accountability is the adoption of processes to hold supervisors and subordinates mutually accountable to each other. While almost all traditional companies have formal performance evaluation systems in which compensation adjustments for subordinates are based on supervisor ratings, few businesses have formal processes where the subordinates rate the supervisors. And for those who do gather subordinate feedback, the ratings are usually part of a 360-degree process that is treated as confidential personal development input and is not factored into the supervisors' compensation adjustments. This sends a clear signal that, while 360-degree evaluations are nice things for organizations to do, they really don't count. The practice of Upward Evaluations radically departs from these established norms by explicitly holding supervisors accountable to their subordinates in a way that influences what bosses are paid.

Upward Evaluations is a practice we created when I became the chief executive of the Blue Cross Blue Shield FEP in early 2002. Believing strongly in the five disciplines of Wiki Management, I wanted to install a process where I would be transparently accountable to all 150 people in the FEP director's office who directly or indirectly reported to me. Because FEP was part of a larger organization that remained very traditional in its management processes, I did not have the liberty to modify or replace the corporate performance evaluation tool. However, because part of the tool provided for the measurement of individual goals, I could propose as one of my performance metrics an evaluation of my effectiveness by the 150 people in the FEP director's office.

To implement this practice, I gathered a diverse committee of about a dozen managers and staff, requesting that they design a tool to measure my effectiveness as a leader. Rather than suggesting the attributes that should be rated, I asked the committee to select the dimensions of my performance that were most important to them. In designing the tool, I specified only two requirements. The first was that no one completing the tool should have to write even one letter on the form—all they would need to do was to circle numbers on a five-point scale. This step protected the anonymity of those completing the forms. The second requirement was that the average rating for each attribute would be calculated using median rather than mean scores. This method was important because, as we extended this practice to other managers, we protected supervisors from retaliation by poor performers who might be on probation. Thus, theoretically in my case, if ten poor performers rated an attribute "1" and the remaining 140 provided a rating of "4," the official score based on the median would be 4.0 as compared to the mean average of 3.8.

The committee was very receptive to the request and designed a survey instrument with forty attributes. We agreed that the committee would be responsible for the distribution, collection, and collation of the evaluations. We also agreed that at no time would I ever see the individual completed forms. I would see only the aggregate median scores for each of the attributes, which I would receive in an e-mail that would be sent to all 150 staff members in the FEP director's office, as well as to my supervisor. According to an agreement I had reached with my supervisor, the results on the evaluation would account for 10 percent of my overall performance evaluation.

The Upward Evaluation is a transparent process that counts. While some managers may be skeptical of a practice that broadly communicates their strengths and weaknesses, my own experience in using this practice is that the results didn't broadcast anything that the staff didn't already know. In fact, I came to see that one of the great benefits of this practice was that it let me know *what everyone knew about me but me*. Becoming aware of my blind spots provided the opportunity to make important changes, but perhaps the greatest benefit of this practice was that I never lost sight of the fact that the people who reported either directly or indirectly to me were not my employees. They were some of my most important customers.

PRACTICE #50: 20 KEY PEOPLE. Of the many different practitioners of Wiki Management we have met in this book, perhaps none is more impressive than W.L. Gore & Associates. The lattice organization that Bill Gore installed when he founded the company—to make sure no one would ever have the authority to kill a good idea or keep a bad idea alive—continues to this day. You may wonder how a company with 9,500 employees and no bosses can achieve the enviable accomplishment of delivering more than fifty years of innovative growth without a single annual loss. The answer is a very simple and powerful practice: 20 Key People.

When Bill Gore decided that he would radically depart from common management practice and build a business without bosses, his biggest practical challenge was coming up with a way to ensure that the workers in his new company would devote their time to projects that made a difference and that they would be incentivized to do more rather than less work. His solution was a very simple and elegant performance evaluation approach that continues to this day. Everyone at Gore is evaluated by at least twenty people and everyone evaluates at least twenty people.[16]

Once a year, every associate is asked to rate his list of peers in a forced ranking from highest to lowest based on the evaluator's overall judgment of each worker's contribution to the company.[17] Gore doesn't tell the associates what criteria to use or prescribe a corporate-wide evaluation tool. According to Terri Kelly, Gore's CEO, "You get a lot of negative behavior when you have narrow metrics that really don't represent the complexities of the business. Instead, we ask our associates to view performance holistically, versus focusing on specific variables."[18]

When the rankings are completed, a cross-functional committee collates the input and compiles the overall rankings, which are then used to set compensation for the next year. At Gore, peer accountability isn't a slogan or a good intention. It's the most important factor in determining what people are paid.

CHAPTER SUMMARY: KEY POINTS

→ Today's challenge of organizing the work of large numbers of people is less about bosses and work assignments and more about leveraging the self-organized efforts of an effective community of peers.

→ In contrast to traditional hierarchies, which limit the interpersonal influence of the many through the ascription of authority, the power structures of wiki-world companies amplify the opportunities for the development of relationships across all the people within an organizational network. The more connections there are, the greater the opportunities for collaboration and innovation, which are the prime drivers for sustained success in fast-changing markets.

→ Self-organized work is more effective than assignments by supervisors because knowledge workers are far more motivated by their standing with their professional peers than they are by pleasing the bosses.

→ Transparency isn't just about everybody knowing everything. It also means that everybody is available to everyone. Without both of these dimensions, true transparency is not possible.

→ The problem of too many people having the authority to kill good ideas needs to be effectively handled if existing organizations want to sustain themselves in an increasingly innovative world. While business leaders may not be able to eliminate the supervisors, a commitment to innovation means they will at least need to eliminate the sovereignty of their supervisors.

Epilogue

W e began this book with a simple premise: A nineteenth-century management model is unsustainable in a twenty-first-century world. The technologies of the Digital Revolution have suddenly transported us into a hyper-connected wiki world where collaborative networks are smarter and faster than top-down hierarchies. The rapid succession of game-changing innovations over the past decade has created an incredible capacity for human ingenuity and accomplishment far beyond our wildest imaginations. And yet the large majority of leaders in both the public and the private sectors fail to leverage this capacity because they are prisoners of a mindset that no longer explains how the world works. It's no wonder that the previously lauded institutions of education and healthcare are now badly broken, our elected politicians can't get anything done, and 70 percent of the *Fortune* 1000 turns over in less than a decade. We clearly have a leadership problem.

Because of their unwillingness to accept the simple premise, the current leaders of our traditional institutions stubbornly double-down on the old ways of managing business by making everyone in their organizations work harder. Unfortunately, despite working people as hard as is humanly possible, the gap in the pace of change between the world and its organizations continues to grow. The only way to close the gap is to work smarter, not harder. And working smarter means following the example of the vanguard companies we met in this book and changing the fundamental ways we manage by getting on the right bus, letting go of an old mindset, and resetting the 3 M's of management.

Hopefully, you have found value in the stories and the practices of the vanguard companies. The leaders of these innovative enterprises are at the forefront of an inevitable management revolution that cannot be thwarted, because the momentum of present-day technology favors those who build networks over those who insist on maintaining hierarchies. While the vanguard companies' ways of managing may be unfamiliar and even counterintuitive, keep in mind that these companies are genuinely loved by their customers, overrepresented on *Fortune*'s list of the "Best Companies to Work For," and more financially sound than their traditional counterparts. The rewards are clearly worth the risks for those who learn how to manage very differently.

I would like to conclude with a final story about the most difficult business mess I faced in my thirty years as a manager and how the disciplines of Wiki Management enabled us to work smarter in handling a major business crisis.

May 8, 2002, was, without a doubt, the worst day of my professional career. When I arrived at the office that Wednesday morning, I was greeted by two managers who informed me that we had a serious problem with the new claims processing system we were building for the Blue Cross Blue Shield FEP. You may recall that FEP is not a vertically integrated business but at the time an alliance of thirty-nine independent companies. Installing a new system meant coordinating thirty-nine simultaneous systems conversions.

Over the previous evening, we had run the first major test of the new claims system, which was scheduled to go live only eight months later in January 2003. The test was a disaster. Nothing was working as expected, and there was an infinite list of problems to be fixed. However, what made this crisis particularly problematic was that while we knew the overall system wasn't working, we had no usable data on the performance of the individual companies. Consequently, we had no idea where to focus our work to correct the problems. We had no analytics to guide the building of an action plan, and without a plan, organizing our efforts would be a misguided shot in the dark. Working harder was not an option; we had to work smarter.

Fortunately for us, we had been practicing Wiki Management for about five years and had used the collective intelligence of our people to guide us in crafting product strategies and improving our regular business processes. While we did not have the ability to use quantifiable data to devise a corrective action plan for our systems problem, we were not totally without access to important information that could guide us to a solution. We had learned through our experience that there are times when diversity trumps ability. Perhaps diversity could help to solve our apparently unsolvable problem.

The following day, I assembled a three-hour meeting of forty members from our central office staff. In addition to people from our systems and operations areas, we had representatives from every functional group and every level in our organization. The full diversity of our business was in the room.

I opened the meeting by explaining that our task was to place the names of every one of the thirty-nine companies in our alliance on one of four flip charts at the front of the room. Each chart had a different color written across the top of the page. Blue meant that the group expected the company would perform well without needing any help from our central office. Green was for companies that were likely to perform well but might need for us to check with them periodically to make sure that they didn't go off course. Yellow designated those companies that would need to be managed very closely because they were likely to be the ones driving the problems we experienced in the test. And, finally, red was for those companies that would likely fail and where no amount of tactical intervention would make a difference because the local CIOs had elected to assign minimal resources to the systems conversion project.

I then reviewed the two rules for color coding each of the companies. The first rule was that no company would be listed on the flip charts until there was unanimous agreement among all forty people. The second rule was that no one should go along with the group just for the sake of moving us along. If even one person truly felt the color designation was wrong, she had an obligation to continue to present her concerns until she was satisfied, because she might be seeing something that no one else recognized. This second rule was most important because it helped ensure that we were tapping into collective intelligence rather than groupthink.

It took us the full three hours to categorize all the companies. When we were done, we had our corrective action plan and a shared understanding about where to focus our work. We left the blue companies alone, periodically checked in with the green companies, and worked very closely with the yellow companies. As for the red companies—there were two of them—a phone call was made to each of their CEOs to put in place the resource commitments necessary to move those organizations onto the yellow list.

In our practice of the disciplines of Wiki Management at FEP, the most important lesson we learned was that when solving complex problems, nobody is smarter than everybody. Because we had the processes to tap into the collective intelligence of our own people, we were able to craft a reliable corrective action plan for our systems crisis. While we felt confident that our plan would work, we were nevertheless surprised by the actual results of our efforts. Unlike the prior systems installation in 1985 that had a year's worth of "bugs" to resolve, when our new claims processing system went live, we did not have a single customer-facing issue. Thanks to the principles and the practices of a twenty-first-century management model, we had achieved a flawless systems conversion.

Whatever role you may have in your company, you can make a difference by selecting and applying the practices in this book that you believe could work in your organization. As you become proficient with the new ways of managing, you will likely design your own novel practices to contribute to the evolving Wiki Management model. After all, the fifty practices in this book are just a starting point. Your most important practices will be the ones that you design to adopt the Wiki Management model for your particular circumstances.

As you explore and experiment with the practices, please keep in mind the key lesson of our final story: In fast-changing times, the most powerful resource in your organization is likely to be the collective intelligence of your own people. If you do your part to learn how to access this resource— by denying people the wherewithal to kill good ideas, gathering everyone in the same room at the same time to build shared understanding, and holding people accountable to each other to deliver what's most important to your customers—you will almost certainly help your organization begin to master the most difficult business challenges of our time. As your mastery grows, you and your colleagues will start to notice that you are keeping up with the pace of change, and you may even be pleasantly surprised to discover that the world is no longer changing faster than your organization.

Notes

CHAPTER 1

1. Brian Hiatt and Evan Serpick, "The Recording Industry's Decline," *RollingStone.com*, posted June 19, 2007.

2. Nathan Furr, "Big Business . . . The End Is Near: Why 70% of the Fortune 1000 Will Be Replaced in a Few Years," *Forbes.com*, posted April 21, 2011.

3. Jim Collins, *Good to Great: Why Some Companies Make the Leap . . . and Others Don't* (New York: HarperCollins, 2001), 41.

4. Ibid.

5. Peter F. Drucker, *Management Challenges for the 21st Century* (New York: HarperBusiness, 1999), 139.

6. Gary Hamel, *What Matters Now: How to Win in a World of Relentless Change, Ferocious Competition, and Unstoppable Innovation* (San Francisco: Jossey-Bass, 2012), 121.

7. Stephen Denning, "The Best-Kept Management Secret on the Planet: Agile," *Forbes.com*, posted April 9, 2012.

8. IBM CEO C-Suite Studies, *Leading Through Connections: Insights from the Global Chief Executive Officer Study*, 2012, 15.

9. Erik H. Erikson, *Childhood and Society* (New York: W.W. Norton, 1950), 147–274.

CHAPTER 2

1. Alan Deutschman, "The Fabric of Creativity," *Fast Company*, December 2004, 54.

2. Gary Hamel, *The Future of Management* (Boston: Harvard Business School Press, 2007), 87.

3. Ibid.

4. Ibid., 88–89.

5. Melanie Mitchell, *Complexity: A Guided Tour* (New York: Oxford University Press, 2009), 13.

6. Margaret J. Wheatley, *Leadership and the New Science: Discovering Order in a Chaotic World* (San Francisco: Berrett-Koehler, 1999), 98.

7. James Surowiecki, *The Wisdom of Crowds: Why the Many Are Smarter than the Few and How Collective Wisdom Shapes Business, Economies, Societies, and Nations* (New York: Doubleday, 2004), 101.

8. Ronald E. Purser and Steven Cabana, *The Self-Managing Organization: How Leading Companies Are Transforming the Work of Teams for Real Impact* (New York: Free Press, 1998), 147–148.

9. Peter F. Drucker, *Management: Tasks, Responsibilities, Practices* (New York: Harper & Row, 1974), 494.

CHAPTER 3

1. Gary Hamel, *What Matters Now: How to Win in a World of Relentless Change, Ferocious Competition, and Unstoppable Innovation* (San Francisco: Jossey-Bass, 2012), 87.

2. Chris McChesney, Sean Covey, and Jim Huling, *The 4 Disciplines of Execution: Achieving Your Wildly Important Goals* (New York: Free Press, 2012), 25.

3. Stephen R. Covey, *The 8th Habit: From Effectiveness to Greatness* (New York: Free Press, 2004), 281.

CHAPTER 4

1. Joseph A. Michelli, *The Zappos Experience: 5 Principles to Inspire, Engage, and Wow* (New York: McGraw-Hill, 2012), 132.

2. Ibid.

3. Michael Hammer, *The Agenda: What Every Business Must Do to Dominate the Decade* (New York: Crown Business, 2001), 179.

4. John Hagel III, John Seely Brown, and Lang Davison, *The Power of Pull: How Small Moves, Smartly Made, Can Set Big Things in Motion* (New York: Basic Books, 2010), 94.

5. A.G. Lafley and Ram Charan, *The Game-Changer: How You Can Drive Revenue and Profit Growth with Innovation* (New York: Crown Business, 2008), 59.

6. Ibid.

7. Michelli, 51.

8. Ibid., 138.

9. Ibid., 107.

10. Ibid., 214.

11. Robert S. Kaplan and David P. Norton, *The Balanced Scorecard: Translating Strategy into Action* (Boston: Harvard Business School Press, 1996).

12. Ibid., 2.

13. Fred Reichheld with Rob Markey, *The Ultimate Question 2.0: How Net Promoter Companies Thrive in a Customer-Driven World* (Boston: Harvard Business Review Press, 2011), 31.

14. Ibid., 25.

15. Ibid., 42.

16. Ibid., 1.

CHAPTER 5

1. Andrew Lih, *The Wikipedia Revolution: How a Bunch of Nobodies Created the World's Greatest Encyclopedia* (New York: Hyperion, 2009), 58.

2. Ibid., 61.

3. Ibid., 45, 64.

4. Firas Khatib, Frank DiMaio, et al., "Crystal Structure of a Monomeric Retroviral Protease Solved by Protein Folding Game Players," *Nature Structural & Molecular Biology*, September 18, 2011.

5. Ibid.

6. James Surowiecki, *The Wisdom of Crowds: Why the Many Are Smarter than the Few and How Collective Wisdom Shapes Business, Economies, Societies, and Nations* (New York: Doubleday, 2004).

7. Ibid., 10.

8. Ibid., xix.

9. Ibid., 74.

10. Don Tapscott and Anthony D. Williams, *Wikinomics: How Mass Collaboration Changes Everything* (New York: Portfolio, 2006), 7.

11. William C. Taylor and Polly LaBarre, *Mavericks at Work: Why the Most Original Minds in Business Win* (New York: HarperCollins, 2006), 63–64.

12. Goldcorp Inc. News Release, "US $575,000 Goldcorp Challenge Awards: World's First 6 Million Ounce Internet Gold Rush Yields High Grade Results," March 12, 2001.

13. Ibid.

14. John Mackey and Raj Sissodia, *Conscious Capitalism: Liberating the Heroic Spirit of Business* (Boston: Harvard Business Review Press, 2013), 89.

15. Ned Smith, "Wisdom of Crowds: Use of Collaboration Software Grows," *BusinessNewsDaily.com*, posted November 10, 2010.

16. Gary Hamel, *The Future of Management* (Boston: Harvard Business School Press, 2007), 230.

CHAPTER 6

1. Andrew Lih, *The Wikipedia Revolution: How a Bunch of Nobodies Created the World's Greatest Encyclopedia* (New York: Hyperion, 2009), 58.

2. Harrison Owen, *Expanding Our Now: The Story of Open Space Technology* (San Francisco: Berrett-Koehler, 1997), 32.

3. Steven Levy, *In the Plex: How Google Thinks, Works, and Shapes Our Lives* (New York: Simon & Schuster, 2011), 130–131.

4. Ibid., 131.

5. Gary Hamel, *The Future of Management* (Boston: Harvard Business School Press, 2007), 116.

6. Kara Swisher, "In Week Two, Marissa Mayer Googifies Yahoo: Free Food! Friday Afternoon All-Hands! New Work Spaces! Fab Swag!" *AllThingsD.com*, posted July 29, 2012.

7. Joseph A. Michelli, *The Zappos Experience: 5 Principles to Inspire, Engage, and Wow* (New York: McGraw-Hill, 2012), 72.

8. Gary Hamel, *What Matters Now: How to Win in a World of Relentless Change, Ferocious Competition, and Unstoppable Innovation* (San Francisco; Jossey-Bass, 2012), 210.

9. Ibid., 213.

10. Ibid., 219.

11. IBM CEO C-Suite Studies, *Leading Through Connections: Insights from the Global Chief Executive Officer Study*, 2012, 6.

12. Ibid.

CHAPTER 7

1. Chris McChesney, Sean Covey, and Jim Huling, *The 4 Disciplines of Execution: Achieving Your Wildly Important Goals* (New York: Free Press, 2012), 12.

2. Walter Isaacson, *Steve Jobs* (New York: Simon & Schuster, 2011), 337.

3. Ibid.

4. Bryce G. Hoffman, *American Icon: Alan Mulally and the Fight to Save Ford Motor Company* (New York: Crown Business, 2012), 55.

5. Ibid., 146.

6. Sanjiv Augustine, *Managing Agile Projects* (Upper Saddle River, NJ: Prentice Hall, 2005), 137.

7. Ibid.

8. McChesney, Covey, and Huling, 6–9.

9. Ibid., 6.

10. Jim Collins, *Good to Great: Why Some Companies Make the Leap . . . and Others Don't* (New York: HarperCollins, 2001), 104.

11. Ibid.

CHAPTER 8

1. David L. Heymann and Guénaël Rodier, "Global Surveillance, National Surveillance, and SARS," *Emerging Infectious Diseases*, February 10, 2004.

2. Ibid.

3. James Surowiecki, *The Wisdom of Crowds: Why the Many Are Smarter than the Few and How Collective Wisdom Shapes Business, Economies, Societies, and Nations* (New York: Doubleday, 2004), 158.

4. Ibid., 159.

5. Ibid., 159–160.

6. Heymann and Rodier.

7. Don Tapscott and Anthony D. Williams, *Wikinomics: How Mass Collaboration Changes Everything* (New York: Portfolio, 2006), 24.

8. Ibid., 81.

9. Ibid.

10. Malcolm Gladwell, *The Tipping Point: How Little Things Can Make a Big Difference* (New York: Little, Brown, 2000), 186.

11. Steven Levy, *In the Plex: How Google Thinks, Works, and Shapes Our Lives* (New York: Simon & Schuster, 2011), 158.

12. Ibid., 159.

13. Ken Auletta, *Googled: The End of the World as We Know It* (New York: Penguin, 2009), 112.

14. Ibid., 286.

15. Bryce G. Hoffman, *American Icon: Alan Mulally and the Fight to Save Ford Motor Company* (New York: Crown Business, 2012), 121.

16. Gary Hamel, *What Matters Now: How to Win in a World of Relentless Change, Ferocious Competition, and Unstoppable Innovation* (San Francisco: Jossey-Bass, 2012), 201.

17. Ibid.

18. Ibid., 202.

Index

accountability changes, 12, 15
Accountability Partners, 185–186
accountability to peers, 28, 49, 59, 66–69,
    71, 171–197
    open source platforms/communities,
      174–176
    peer hiring process, 110–111
    peers over supervisors, 176–178
    practices, 180–196
    scientific research and, 171–174
    Solo/Team Balanced Goals, 145–147
    transparency over control, 178–180
    vanguard companies, 176–178
adaptive strategy, 10
agendas, 135–137, 164, 189–191
Agile software developers, 18–20, 81–82,
    131–133, 161
agile teams, 16–17, 81–82
Agrarian Age, 31–32, 55
Airbus Industrie, 158
airlines, 75–78, 88, 158
Amazon, 5, 103–104
Amelio, Gil, 158

American League Baseball, 149–153
Apple, 4, 14, 54, 57–58, 93–94, 112,
    157–158
Ask the Audience, 85–86
Augustine, Sanjiv, 161
automobile industry, 30, 39–40, 56,
    158–159, 191–192
Autonomous Peer Input, 192–193

Bain & Company, 94–95
Balanced Scorecards, 92–93, 166
baseball, 149–153
Beane, Billy, 150–153
Best Buy, 120–121
bird flight, 38
Blackberry, 57–58
Blockbuster, 4–5, 6
Blue Cross Blue Shield Federal
      Employee Program (FEP)
    Consensus High Performers, 121–122
    Cross-Functional Goals, 143–145
    Customer Proxies, 90
    Deep Dives, 163–165

EPO (Exclusive Provider Option)
    negotiations, 113–114
National Football League (NFL)
    comparison, 123–124
The One Number, 168–169
On-the-Spot Agendas, 189–190
Open Space meetings, 136–137
shared understanding over
    compliance, 126
Solo/Team Balanced Goals, 146–147
Top Four Performance Drivers,
    166–167
Town Hall Conference Calls,
    137–139
Upward Evaluations, 194–195
Wiki Management impact in crisis,
    200–203
Work-Thru sessions, 63–65, 123–126
Boeing Commercial Airplanes Group,
    158
bookstores, 5, 6, 163
Borders, 5, 6
Brin, Sergey, 53–54, 139–140, 183–185
Business 2.0, 47
business models, 21–22

Carroll, Chuck, 29
Carroll, Dave, 75–78, 88
Centers for Disease Control and
    Prevention (CDC), 172
change
    accelerating, 8, 13–16, 17, 23–24,
        154–155, 180
    accountability, 12, 15
    exponential, 13–17
    incremental, 3–4, 8, 17
    mindset, 31–34
    Moore's Law and, 13–16
    order versus chaos and, 128–131, 178
    paradigm shift, 34–36, 39–40, 70
    resetting 3 M's, 53–73
chaos, order versus, 128–131, 178
China, SARS outbreak, 171–174
Choose Your Colleagues, 109–111
Circuit City, 5, 6

Clarifying Questions, 90–91
classified advertising, 35
Collaboration Software, 115–116
Colleague Letters of Understanding
    (CLOU), 142–143
Collective Forecasts, 120–121
collective intelligence, 43, 48, 64–65,
    99–122
    aggregating and leveraging, 102–104,
        133
    electronic learning platforms in,
        40–41, 42, 53–55, 94, 103–104, 108
    games and contests, 101–102, 104–107,
        108, 116–117, 120–121
    leading by facilitation, 19, 24, 42–43,
        46, 49, 60–62, 69, 72, 86, 111–112,
        136–137
    networks over hierarchies, 38,
        102–103, 108–109
    open source platforms and, 99–101,
        104–107
    practices in, 109–122
    scientific research and, 101–102, 116
    Simple Rules, 155–157
    Wiki Management in crisis situation,
        200–203
    Wikipedia and, 40, 46, 99–101, 108,
        140
    wisdom of crowds in, 38, 102–103,
        108–109, 120–121
Collins, Jim, 5, 6, 167
color coding, 191–192, 201–203
command-and-control structure, 18,
    32–34, 44, 60, 108, 112
complex adaptive systems, 36–43
    examples of, 39–43
    organizing principles of, 36–39,
        43–45
    see also Wiki Management
complexity, 9–11, 13–16, 36, 178
connectivity, 11–16, 20–24
consensus, 121–122, 125–126
Consensus High Performers, 121–122
contests and games, 101–102, 104–107,
    108, 116–117, 120–121

control
    controls versus, 43–45
    order versus chaos, 128–131, 178
    transparency over, 178–180
    see also hierarchical organizations
Cook, Scott, 95
corporate knowledge management
    systems, 116
corporate mission statements, 21, 127
Covey, Stephen, 67
Craigslist, 35
creativity, 10–11, 17, 129–131, 134–135
Cross-Functional Goals, 143–145
cross-functional processes, 9, 12, 18–20,
    127, 143–145
cruise industry, 165–166
Cunningham, Ward, 18, 99–100, 131–
    132
customer-centric approach, 10, 47–48,
    75–97
    customer service in, 75–79, 84–85,
        86–87, 89
    customers over bosses in, 78–79
    practices in, 82–96
    serendipity over planning in, 79–82
    social media in, 69–70, 75–77, 87–89
Customer Proxies, 90

Daily Stand-Up Meetings, 161
Deep Dives, 162–166
DeHart, Jacob, 85–86
Denning, Stephen, 18
Detach from Outcome, 112–114
Detroit Tigers, 150
Digital Age/Revolution, 7–24, 40, 42–43,
    60–61, 80, 108–109, 111, 116
    accelerating change and, 8, 13–16, 17,
        23–24, 154–155, 180
    Agile Manifesto in, 18–20
    connectivity in, 11–16, 20–24
    evolution of technology, 55–57
    exponential change and, 16–17
    increasing complexity and, 9–11,
        13–16
    lattice organizations and, 27–29, 46

    managing the future, 16–17
    mass collaboration in, 11–16, 20–24,
        60–61
    mindset of, 33–34
    Moore's Law and, 13–16
    power dynamics shift and, 17–18
    values rebalancing in, 20–24
    see also Wiki Management
disease control, 171–174
disengagement, 126–127
Dish Network, 4–5
diversity of opinion, 102, 109, 134
Drucker, Peter, 7, 45
DuPont Company, 27
DynaTAC phone, 57–58

eBay, 103–104
efficiency, 6–7
electronic learning platforms, 40–41, 42,
    53–55, 94, 103–104
The Elegant Set, 117–118
Encyclopedia Britannica, 101
enterprise tools, 116
Erikson, Erik, 22
Expanding Our Now (Owen), 137

Facebook, 69–70, 77, 88
facilitative leadership, 19, 24, 42–43, 46,
    49, 60–62, 69, 72, 86, 111–112,
    136–137
failure, tolerance for, 10
Fannie Mae, 5
financial statements
    Balanced Scorecards, 92–93, 166
    lagging indicators, 92–93, 153, 154
    Teach the Numbers, 141–142
Foldit, 101–102, 116, 117
football, 123–124
Forbes.com, 5
Ford Motor Company, 158–159, 191–192
Fortune magazine
    Fortune 1000 replacement rate, 5
    100 "Best Companies to Work For"
        list, 28, 54, 59, 111, 200
FranklinCovey, 67, 162–163

Free Meals, 140–141
Fresno First Bank, 141–142
Furr, Nathan, 5

games and contests, 101–102, 104–107,
     108, 116–117, 120–121
Gates, Bill, 81
Gibson, William, 16
Global Public Health Intelligence
     Network (GPHIN), 171–174
goals, 67–69, 95–96
     Cross-Functional, 143–145
     Solo/Team Balanced Goals, 145–147
Goldcorp Inc., 104–107, 108, 116
Google, 21
     collective intelligence and, 40–41, 42,
          53–55, 104, 108
     Free Meals, 140–141
     manager role in, 41–42
     origins of, 20
     PageRank algorithm, 40–41, 42,
          53–55, 104, 108
     planning horizon of, 81–82
     60:1 Rule, 183–184
     team building and, 10
     TGIF webcasts, 139–140
     20% Rule, 184–185
Gore, Bill, 27–29, 30, 46, 181, 182,
     195–196
Gore-Tex, 28
Great Depression, 5
Great Recession, 30, 141–142
groupthink, 63, 102, 202

Hamel, Gary, 16
Hammer, Michael, 78
Harrington, Mike, 134–135
hierarchical organizations, 6–7, 8, 15,
     18–20, 23, 27–28, 32–34, 37, 43–45,
     56, 60, 108–109, 179–180, 182
high engagement environment, 126–127
Hong Kong University, 172
human relations movement, 20, 56–57

IBM, 20–21, 39–40, 89, 145, 175–176
independent thinking, 102, 109

Industrial Age/Revolution, 9, 11, 32, 43,
     55, 56, 80, 106, 107, 182
innovation
     components of, 9–11
     Free Meals, 140–141
     Innovation Jams, 89
     managing, 57–58
     Net Promoter Score, 93–95
     20% Rule, 184–185
Intel, 13–14
Internet
     connectivity and, 11–16, 20–24, 33–34
     electronic learning platforms and,
          40–41, 42, 53–55, 94, 103–104
     mass collaboration and, 11–16, 20–24
     music recording industry and, 3–4, 6,
          8, 69, 112, 133, 134, 154
     online games and contests, 101–102,
          104–107, 108, 116–117
     search engines, 53–55
Intuit, 95
iPhone, 54, 57–58
iTunes, 4, 112
"ivory tower" syndrome, 134

Jobs, Steve, 9–11, 157–158
Johnson & Johnson, 39–40
Join the Chat, 87–89

Kaplan, Robert, 92–93
Kelly, Terri, 29, 196
Khatib, Firas, 101–102, 116
Kill the Killer, 180–182
Kovitz, Ben, 99–101

lagging indicators, 92–93, 153, 154
Lamarr, Zaz, 77–78, 79, 87
lattice organizations, 27–29, 46, 176–177,
     181–182, 195–196
Law of Two Feet, 136
Lead by Facilitation, 111–112
Leadership Team Guests, 133–134
leading indicators, 152–153, 154–155
lean management, 30
LEGO, 83–84
Let's Play a Game, 116–117

Liberating Structures, 118–120
LinkedIn, 88
Linux, 11, 40, 41, 105, 174–176
Lipmanowicz, Henri, 118–119
local knowledge, 102, 109

Mackey, John, 110, 111
Major League Baseball, 149–153
management
    accountability changes and, 12, 15
    Agile Manifesto, 18–20
    agile teams, 16–17
    exponential change and, 13–17
    "good-to-great" businesses
        (J. Collins), 5, 6–7
    of innovation, 57–58
    innovative approach to, 9–11
    in lattice organizations, 27–28, 46,
        176–177, 181–182, 195–196
    as new discipline, 11, 32
    participative, 20, 56–57
    resetting 3 M's, 53–73
    Scientific, 6–7
    top-down hierarchies in, 6–7, 8, 15,
        18–20, 23, 27–28, 32–34, 37, 43–45,
        56, 60, 108–109, 179–180, 182
    Toyota Way, 30
    traditional approach to, 6–7, 8,
        18–20, 21–23, 27–28, 32–34,
        43–45, 49–50, 69–71
    see also Wiki Management
management models, 21–22
managers/manager resetting, 82–87,
        109–114, 131–134, 155–159,
        180–187
    Accountability Partners, 185–186
    Ask the Audience, 85–86
    Choose Your Colleagues, 109–111
    collaborative managers, 41–45, 59,
        60–61, 64–65, 71
    customer service and, 75–79, 84–85
    Detach from Outcome, 112–114
    Kill the Killer, 180–182
    Lead by Facilitation, 111–112
    Leadership Team Guests, 133–134
    Manage the Container, 131–133

Meet the Customer, 84–85
No More Than Four, 157–159
One and Done, 86–87
Simple Rules, 155–157
60:1 Rule, 183–184
Temporary Leaders, 186–187
Think Outside-In, 82–84
20% Rule, 184–185
Manage the Container, 131–133
Managing Agile Projects (Augustine), 161
Maslow, Abraham, 20
mass collaboration, 11–16, 20–24, 60–61
    collaborative networks in, 17
    cross-functional processes and, 9, 12
Mayer, Marissa, 141, 185
McCandless, Keith, 118–119
McEwen, Rob, 104–107, 116
McGregor, Douglas, 20
measures/performance driver resetting,
        48, 92–96, 120–122, 141–147,
        149–170, 191–196
    accelerating change and, 154–155
    Autonomous Peer Input, 192–193
    Balanced Scorecards, 92–93, 166
    bonuses, 110–111
    Colleague Letters of Understanding
        (CLOU), 142–143
    Collective Forecasts, 120–121
    Consensus High Performers, 121–122
    Cross-Functional Goals, 143–145
    cross-team measures, 59, 66–69, 71
    games and contests, 101–102, 104–107,
        120–121
    lagging indicators, 92–93, 153, 154
    leading indicators, 152–153, 154–155
    Major League Baseball, 149–153
    Net Promoter Score, 93–95, 96
    No More Than Four, 157–159
    The One Number, 167–169
    practices, 155–169
    Results-Based/Values-Based Goals,
        95–96
    Solo/Team Balanced Goals, 145–147
    Teach the Numbers, 141–142
    Top Four Performance Drivers,
        166–167

measures/performance driver resetting
(continued)
 True Colors, 191–192
 20 Key People, 195–196
 Upward Evaluations, 193–195
meetings/meeting resetting, 62–65,
  87–91, 115–120, 134–141, 159–166,
  187–191
 Clarifying Questions, 90–91
 Collaboration Software, 115–116
 committee-style, 62–63, 65
 Customer Proxies, 90
 Daily Stand-Up Meetings, 161
 Deep Dives, 162–166
 The Elegant Set, 117–118
 Free Meals, 140–141
 games and contests, 116–117
 Innovation Jams, 89
 Join the Chat, 87–89
 Let's Play a Game, 116–117
 Milestone Timelines, 187–189
 online forums, 89
 On-the-Spot Agendas, 189–191
 Open Space Meetings, 42, 135–137
 Rotating Tables, 159–161
 Sit by Project, 134–135
 sprint meetings, 132–133
 TGIF webcasts, 139–140
 Town Hall Conference Calls,
  137–139
 25/10 Crowd Sourcing, 118–119
 virtual meetings, 87–89
 Wise Crowds, 119–120
 see also open conversations
Meet the Customer, 84–85
micromanagement, 156, 183–184
Microsoft, 81, 116, 134–135, 175
Milestone Timelines, 187–189
millennial generation, 33, 133, 134
mindsets, 27–51
 changes in, 31–34
 coexistence of fading and emerging,
  35–36
 complex adaptive systems, 36–43
 Digital Revolution and, 33–34

five disciplines, 47–49
 language and, 31
 letting go of old, 27–29, 43–47, 50
 nature of, 30
 paradigm shift, 34–36, 39–40, 70
 power of, 30–34
Mitchell, Melanie, 36
mobile phone industry, 57–58
Moneyball (film), 150
Moore, Gordon, 13–14
Moore's Law, 13–16
Morning Star, 142–143, 181
Motorola, 57–58
Mulally, Alan, 158–159, 191–192
music recording industry, 3–4, 6, 8, 69,
  112, 133, 134, 154, 163

Napster, 3–4, 112
National Football League (NFL),
  123–124
National League Baseball, 149–153
Netflix, 4–5
Net Promoter Score, 93–95, 96
networked-based management model,
  27–28
Newell, Gabe, 134–135
Newmark, Craig, 35
newspaper industry, 35
New York Yankees, 150
Nickell, Nake, 85–86
Nokia, 57–58
No More Than Four, 157–159
Norton, David, 92–93
Nupedia, 99–101, 132

Oakland Athletics, 150–153
objectives, 68–69
One and Done, 86–87
The One Number, 167–169
online forums, 89
On-the-Spot Agendas, 189–191
open conversations, 42, 46, 48, 59,
  115–116, 123–147
 consensus and, 125–126
 emergent over directed, 128–129

good surprises/bad surprises, 129–131
order versus chaos, 128–131
practices, 131–147
shared understanding over
    compliance, 126–127
Work-Thru sessions, 63–65, 123–126
open source platforms/communities, 46
accountability to peers, 174–176
Goldcorp Challenge, 104–107, 108,
    116
Manage the Container, 131–133
see also Linux; Wikipedia
Open Space Meetings, 42, 135–137
operating models, 21–22
order, chaos versus, 128–131, 178
organizational design, 40–41
organizational development, 22
organization charts, 32–34
Owen, Harrison, 135–137

Page, Larry, 53–54, 139–140, 183–185
PageRank algorithm (Google), 40–41,
    42, 53–55, 104
paradigm shift, 34–36, 39–40, 70
participative management, 20, 56–57
passenger-ship industry, 165–166
peer accountability, see accountability
    to peers
performance drivers, see measures/
    performance driver resetting
planning
    planning horizons in, 81–82
    serendipity over, 79–82
    True Colors in Business Plan Review
        (BPR), 191–192
Post-It Notes, 184
power dynamics, 17–18
priorities, 67–69
problem-solving skills, escalating
    complexity and, 9–11
Procter & Gamble, 39–40
productivity, 6–7

Reichheld, Fred, 94–95
Research in Motion, 57–58

resilience, 17
Results-Based/Values-Based goals,
    95–96
Rotating Tables, 159–161

Sanger, Larry, 99–101, 132
Schmidt, Eric, 139–140
Schwaber, Ken, 18
Scientific Management, 6–7
scientific research, 101–102, 116,
    171–174
Scrum, 18–19
selective consultation, 20
self-organizing systems, 27–29, 34, 36–37,
    41–43, 44–45, 60–61, 142–143,
    177–178, 181–182
serendipity
    Free Meals and, 140–141
    nature of, 80–81
    planning over, 79–82
    Sit by Project and, 134–135
Severts, Jeff, 120–121
shared understanding
    compliance versus, 126–127
    Milestone Timelines, 187–189
    see also open conversations
SharePoint Web application platform,
    116
Simple Rules, 155–157
Sit by Project, 134–135
60:1 Rule, 183–184
social media, 69–70, 75–77, 87–89,
    115–116
software development
    Agile Manifesto and, 18–20, 82,
        131–133
    Manage the Container, 131–133
Solo/Team Balanced Goals, 145–147
sprints, 132–133
Star performers, 108–109
Stone Age, 55
Surowiecki, James, 38, 102–103, 108–109,
    120–121
surprises, 129–131
Sutherland, Jeff, 18

Taylor, Bob, 76
Taylor, Frederick Winslow, 6–7
Taylor Guitars, 76, 88
Teach the Numbers, 141–142
team building, 10
Temporary Leaders, 186–187
TGIF webcasts, 139–140
Theory X, 20
Theory Y, 20
Think Outside-In, 82–84
Threadless, 85–86
360-degree evaluations, 193–194
3M, 184
3Ms, 39–40, 53–73
    see also managers/manager resetting;
        measures/performance driver
        resetting; meetings/meeting
        resetting
time and motion studies, 6–7
top-down hierarchies, 6–7, 8, 15, 18–20,
    23, 27–28, 32–34, 37, 43–45, 56, 60,
    108–109
Top Four Performance Drivers, 166–167
Torvalds, Linus, 41, 46, 105, 174–176
Town Hall Conference Calls, 137–139
Toyota, 30, 39–40, 158
transparency
    color coding and, 191–192, 201–203
    control and, 178–180
True Colors, 191–192
turf battles, 179, 190
25/10 Crowd Sourcing, 118–119
20 Key People, 195–196
20% Rule, 184–185
Twitter, 69–70, 77, 88, 89, 115–116

United Airlines, 75–76, 77, 78, 88
University of Washington, 101–102
Upward Evaluations, 193–195

values, 20–24, 95–96
    empowering employees through,
        20–21
    organizational development and, 22

paradoxical, 21–23
shifts in, 23–24, 49–50
Valve, 134–135, 181
Verizon, 112
video rental industry, 4–5, 6, 163

W. L. Gore & Associates, 20, 27–29, 30,
    39–40, 46, 179, 181, 182, 186–187,
    195–196
Wales, Jimmy, 41, 46, 99–101, 111, 132
Walgreen's, 167–168
Walpole, Horace, 80–81
Wheatley, Margaret, 37
whirlwind, 162–163
Whitsell, Rick, 141–142
Whole Foods, 110–111
Wiki Management, 39–43
    accountability to peers in, 28, 49, 59,
        66–69, 71, 171–197
    Agile Manifesto and, 18–20
    collective intelligence in, 40–41, 43,
        48, 53–55, 64–65, 99–122
    components of, 17, 23, 40–43, 47–49
    content versus context and, 45–47
    controls versus control and, 43–45
    creative meetings, 62–65, 71, see also
        meetings/meeting resetting
    crisis application, 200–203
    cross-team measures, 59, 66–69, 71,
        see also measures/performance
        driver resetting
    customer-centric approach in, 47–48,
        69–70, 75–97
    examples of, 39–40
    key ideas of, 40–43
    manager role in, 41–45, 59, 60–61,
        64–65, 71, see also managers/
        manager resetting
    nature of wiki world, 8
    open conversations in, 42, 46, 48, 59,
        63–65, 123–147
    overview, 71
    resetting 3 M's, 53–73
    resistance to change, 39–40

self-organizing systems in, 41–43,
    44–45, 60–61
transition from traditional manage-
    ment to, 43–45, 49–50, 69–71
vanguard companies, 16, 17, 30,
    39–41, 94–95, 108, 112, 157, 163,
    176–178, 200
Wikipedia, 11, 18
    collective intelligence and, 40, 46,
        99–101, 108, 140
    manager role in, 41
    Manage the Container, 132–133
    origins and development of, 99–101,
        115, 140
    performance drivers and, 153
    Simple Rules, 155–157
WikiWikiWeb site, 99–100, 131–132
wiki world
    emergence of, 33–34
    millennial generation and, 33
    mindset of, 33–34

nature of, 8, 17, 23, 67–68
new technologies of, 29
origins of wiki, 18, 20, 99–100,
    131–132
wiki, defined, 8, 115
Wisdom of Crowds, The (Surowiecki), 38,
    102–103, 108–109, 120–121
Wise Crowds, 119–120
Work-Thru sessions, 63–65,
    123–126
World Health Organization
    (WHO), 171–174

Yahoo, 53–54, 141, 185
Yammer, 115–116
YouTube, 69–70, 76–77, 88

Zappos, 21
    customer service, 77–78, 79, 84–85,
        86–87, 89
    Free Meals, 141